HOW HOUSING ALLOWANCES WORK
Integrated Findings from the Experimental Housing Allowance Program

DAVID B. CARLSON
JOHN D. HEINBERG

249-3

February 1978

THE URBAN INSTITUTE
WASHINGTON, D.C.

The research forming the basis for this publication was funded by the Office of Policy Development and Research, U.S. Department of Housing and Urban Development, through Contract H-2162R.

ISBN 87766-215-0

UI 249-3

PLEASE REFER TO URI 21300 WHEN ORDERING

Available from:

Publications Office
The Urban Institute
2100 M Street, N.W.
Washington, D.C. 20037

List price: $4.00

A/78/1500

PREFACE

This paper is part of the Integrated Analysis of the Experimental Housing Allowance Program (EHAP). It was developed in consultation with the Housing Research Division, Office of Policy Development and Research, U.S. Department of Housing and Urban Development to provide a comprehensive, coherent picture of what has been learned to date from EHAP research. A special effort has therefore been made to present this EHAP experience with a general audience in mind. For the reader who seeks a more technical discussion, the Selected Bibliography at the end of this document lists publications containing more detailed treatments of individual topics.

We would like to express our appreciation, without thereby implying any responsibility for the paper, to those individuals who commented on earlier drafts. In particular, Terrence Connell of HUD worked closely with us during all stages of the paper's development. A number of useful comments--including the recommendation to extend our coverage to reflect all the analysis of first-year experience in the Demand Experiment--were received at a meeting of an independent review panel on EHAP research held in July 1977. Katharine Lyall and Henry Schechter, present at that meeting, had been asked to prepare review comments and offered especially helpful advice. Helen Bakeman of Abt Associates, Incorporated, and Thomas Kingsley of The Rand Corporation also assisted in the review process, reflecting the perspectives of the three EHAP experiments.

Besides our own work, this paper draws on the work of Abt Associates, Incorporated, and The Rand Corporation. In addition to published or draft analysis reports, requested tabulations based on Housing Allowance Office records in the Supply Experiment were prepared by Paul Tebbets of Rand. Larry Kozimor, also of Rand, provided data on rent expenditures of recipient households in the two Supply sites.

Members of The Urban Institute staff who contributed in many ways to the writing of this paper through early drafts of sections and review include Verna Alburger, Frank Cronin, Jeanne Goedert, Jack Goodman, Larry Ozanne, Ronald Sepanik, Grace Taher, John Trutko, Jean Vanski and James Zais. Morton Isler, Director of the Housing Studies Program, provided major direction by thorough and insightful review of the work. Elizabeth Bernsten, Margaret Drury, Timmy Napolitano, Ann Schnare, Raymond Struyk (now at HUD) and Lorene Yap also reviewed an earlier draft. Karen Brown edited the paper. It was typed quickly and accurately by Beverly Caldwell and Frances Collins.

CONTENTS

APPENDIXES

LIST OF TABLES AND FIGURES

Tables

LIST OF TABLES AND FIGURES (continued)

Figures

SUMMARY

This paper draws on evidence to date from the Experimental Housing Allowance Program (EHAP) and is organized in terms of major program outcomes that EHAP was designed to address:

- How and why families participate in housing allowance programs.
- How families are assisted by such programs.
- The effects of programs on housing markets and communities.
- Overall program administration and costs, including the extrapolation of those costs to a national level.

EHAP contains three component experiments, each of which pertains to distinct research objectives related to these outcomes: (1) a Demand Experiment, to observe how allowances are used by program participants; (2) a Supply Experiment, to investigate the effects of an open-enrollment allowance program on housing markets and prices; and (3) an Administrative Agency Experiment, to provide information on various procedures for managing an allowance program. The program design also includes a fourth research component, the Integrated Analysis, which seeks (1) to analyze and communicate the EHAP experience as a total entity--an integrated whole, but one that takes account of the individual experimental settings and findings as well as analysis across experimental lines--and (2) to interpret how the experience can be generalized appropriately for use in the development of national housing policy.

In addition to current EHAP findings, this paper contains a comprehensive review of the background and scope of EHAP, a report on program operations and an annotated bibliography of selected research materials developed to date.

Participation in Housing Allowance Programs

One of EHAP's important objectives is to develop an understanding of the factors influencing the decisions of lower-income households concerning participation in housing allowance programs. Housing allowances in EHAP are monthly payments provided directly to families that have been determined to be unable to afford a decent home in a suitable living environment. Becoming a housing allowance recipient in EHAP is a two-step process: a low-income household learns about the program, applies and is certified as an enrollee; once enrolled, the family must live in a unit that meets the program's housing requirements--housing standards or minimum rent--in order to receive allowance payments.

Three factors particularly seem to affect whether a family enrolls: (1) awareness of the program, (2) the degree to which a family might perceive "welfare stigma" and (3) the amount of allowance payments anticipated. More intensive outreach procedures were successful in raising enrollment levels for some groups (e.g., the elderly and the working poor).

To become a recipient, an enrolled family needs to live in a unit that meets program housing requirements. In most cases, these involve housing quality standards. So the existence and stringency of the program housing standards themselves, which vary considerably among different parts of EHAP, affect how enrollees become recipients. Evidence indicates that three factors related to the local housing market are also involved in this process: (1) the quality of the area's housing; (2) the inclination of households to move and (3) availability of program-acceptable units to enrollees, especially as influenced by rental vacancy rates and patterns of residential segregation.

The interplay of forces between the EHAP participation process and local housing market conditions affected different families in different ways, for instance:

- Minority households generally enrolled at higher rates than non-minorities. The housing of minority families was usually of poorer quality and they were less satisfied with their housing conditions and neighborhoods. Some minority families with this poor quality housing had difficulty meeting EHAP's housing requirements and becoming recipients. Thus minority households who enrolled generally attained recipient status at lower rates than did non-minorities.
- Elderly households had lower enrollment rates because they generally were less aware of the program and seemed more reluctant to apply even if they heard of it. More intensive outreach helped boost elderly enrollment, and elderly families who enrolled were generally more likely than non-elderly families to meet housing requirements and become recipients.
- Welfare families in general enrolled at higher rates than others; their awareness of the program was strongly associated with referrals from other agencies. Once enrolled, they were about as successful in becoming recipients as were the working poor (i.e., low-income families not receiving welfare benefits).
- The working poor were evidently bothered by a "welfare stigma" they attached to allowances. This factor appeared to keep their enrollment lower than welfare families. There is some evidence, however, that media outreach especially oriented to

the working poor is effective in raising their enrollment rate.

- Homeowners, eligible only in the two Supply Experiment sites, Green Bay and South Bend, enrolled at much lower rates than did renters. However, once enrolled, homeowners became recipients at higher rates than renters. Some homeowners who perceived that they would have problems meeting program housing standards apparently chose not to enroll.
- Female-headed families enrolled at higher rates than male-headed families. Once enrolled, families with female heads became recipients at about the same rate as families with male heads.

How Participants Are Assisted by Housing Allowance Programs

Housing allowance payments provided different patterns of benefits to participating families, depending principally upon how they met program housing requirements: some families met these requirements at enrollment; others had to move or upgrade their dwellings. Throughout EHAP to date, about half the participating families met the requirements at enrollment.

Evidence from the Demand Experiment indicates that families already meeting housing requirements at enrollment spent their allowances much as they would have any other income. There was, however, another effect on housing conditions for this group of families that is perceived most clearly in the Supply Experiment: after enrollment, some families might have either moved to a substandard unit or let their units fall below program standards if it had not been for the housing standards.

For the other half of participant families, those whose original dwelling did not meet program housing requirements, allowances were associated with major changes in housing expenditures. For all such families in the Demand Experiment sites, housing expenditures rose an estimated average of 20 percent in the first year, due to actions that were induced by the allowance program. Most of this increase was attributable to households that moved.

A trade-off exists, however, between the effects of program housing requirements on the housing circumstances of participants and the effects of requirements on how families participate. The existence and stringency of program housing requirements influence positively the housing expenditure patterns of some participants but they also affect negatively the number of program-eligible families who are willing and able to participate.

In the Administrative Agency Experiment and Supply Experiment sites only gross (unadjusted) measures of housing expenditure changes are currently available. Subsequent analysis should yield better measures of program-induced effects, but evidence to date in these two experiments indicates important differences. In the Administrative Agency Experiment sites, more participants moved than in the Demand sites and the gross increase in expenditures was greater. In the Supply Experiment, however, fewer renter participants have moved and the gross rent increase was smaller after roughly one year of participant experience.

For families that moved or upgraded, housing conditions were improved in varying degrees. In the Demand sites, it was estimated that less than half of the recipients that lived in housing that met program housing requirements after one year but not at enrollment were induced to do so by the program. This group constituted about 20 percent of all recipients.

About one-third of all housing units of participants at the Supply Experiment sites have undergone some form of upgrading to date, although most of it is modest. In both Supply sites, the median "out-of-pocket" cost per dwelling unit for repairs to bring those dwellings up to standard was about $10 per unit, although most of the labor was supplied by the tenant or the landlord/owner. More extensive repairs have, however, been reported for some units.

Overcrowded housing conditions were also affected by EHAP. The Administrative Agency Experiment offers evidence that some recipients--predominantly larger families of five or more persons--were able to reduce crowding by moving to larger units.

Data from EHAP indicate that families were not generally induced to move any more often than they would have ordinarily. Moreover, those who moved appeared to move in established geographic patterns. More conclusive statements will be possible as more data become available. Thus far, however, there is no statistically significant evidence from EHAP that housing allowances have altered patterns of racial and ethnic settlement.

In addition to possible effects on mobility rates and racial and ethnic concentration, it is important to understand whether participants moved to neighborhoods of better quality. Housing allowance programs tested in EHAP provide no direct incentive for neighborhood improvements by recipients; program housing requirements do not include such items. Evidence to date indicates that EHAP households have moved, on average, to neighborhoods of better quality, but that their experience in this regard has been no different than that of similar households not receiving allowances.

Finally, all recipient families were able to pay smaller percentages of their pre-allowance incomes for rent. The families that enrolled were paying relatively high percentages of gross income for rent (an average of 42 percent in the Administrative Agency Experiment sites) before receiving the allowances. Allowances have constituted a major addition to the net incomes of participants--roughly 25 percent on average.

The Effects of a Housing Allowance on Markets and Communities

A key concern about housing allowances is whether or not they would merely serve to raise rents for lower-income families, without improving housing quality. EHAP's Supply Experiment is measuring these effects at two sites, Green Bay and South Bend, and to date there is no evidence of program-induced price inflation. There appear to be two major factors contributing to this result: (1) participation levels have been lower than anticipated and (2) participants have increased their housing expenditures by only a fraction of the payments they received. Analysis is continuing; it is still too early to know with certainty that there will be no program-induced price increases.

EHAP has been generally well received in all sites. In South Bend, those suburban communities that had originally refused to take part in the program subsequently have agreed to participate. In both South Bend and Green Bay, community resources have been made available to complement the allowance program; local governments in these sites have allocated funds for home improvement loans and housing rehabilitation.

Housing Allowance Program Administration and Costs

The two major cost elements under analysis in EHAP are administrative costs and transfer costs--the costs of allowance payments.

The Administrative Agency Experiment was specifically designed to measure management costs for housing allowances. Variations in management procedures among the eight Administrative Agency Experiment agencies led to considerable variations both in intake costs--what it cost to bring families into the program--and maintenance costs--what it cost to maintain families in the program. Intake costs per recipient family (adjusted for site differences in family drop-outs during intake) varied from \$151 to \$292 across the eight sites (median of \$225 per year); maintenance costs, from \$129 to \$322 (median of \$205 per year). When the intake costs are amortized over five years--the average length of time that participating families were assumed to remain in the program--the annual amortized intake figure is \$45 per year for each family. Adding this to the \$205 per year that it costs to maintain a family in the experiment, the total management cost would be \$250 per family annually. Procedural variations among agencies did affect these figures, particularly in the areas of outreach, inspections and the provision of services.

Transfer costs--allowance payments--varied primarily because of use of a different income definition in the Demand Experiment, variations in the estimated cost of adequate housing at each site and the different types of tenure included in each experiment: the Supply Experiment allows homeowner participation, whereas the other two experiments were limited to renters. The average monthly payment in the eight Administrative Agency Experiment sites was about \$80. Payments in Phoenix averaged \$78 per family per month; in Pittsburgh, \$50. As of August 1977, payments averaged \$75 per month in Green Bay, and in South Bend, \$70.

Extrapolating EHAP experience to date through simulation modeling to a possible national-level allowance program has involved assuming a program most like the Supply Experiment of EHAP (e.g., open enrollment, with both homeowners and renters eligible), similar participation levels (no more than 40 percent of all eligible households) and no increases in costs due to program-induced inflation. Based on these assumptions, the analysis indicates that about 7.2 million households would participate in a national program. Transfer payments would average about $65 per month for each recipient household--$56 for homeowners and $69 for renters. The total allowance costs per year would be about $5.7 billion in 1976 dollars when the program reaches steady state. Analysis of alternative administrative structures for a national-level housing program does not yet permit estimates of costs. Based on administrative cost experience and analysis from the Administrative Agency Experiment, however, per-family administrative costs would average about $20 monthly. For the 7.2 million participants indicated above, this would imply total administrative costs of $1.7 billion annually. This experience reflects small-scale programs at the agency level and the development of an administrative structure separate from other welfare-system programs--approaches that might not be reflected in a national-level program. Based on specific assumptions regarding EHAP evidence to date, however, total program costs for the nation as a whole, adding management and allowance costs, would be $7.4 billion or about $85 per month for every recipient family.

Chapter I.
INTRODUCTION

This paper presents a synthesis of findings from more than four years of testing the housing allowance concept through the operation of the Experimental Housing Allowance Program. It reflects program operations and analysis completed through August 1977.[1]

This paper is designed to capture a major milestone in interim reporting of findings based on important stages of progress in the three experimental components of EHAP. The Administrative Agency Experiment has now completed its analysis. Demand Experiment evidence reflects completion of all analysis of the first year of household responses to housing allowances. And the Supply Experiment, in its Third Annual Report, for the first time has presented major research findings and compared them across Supply sites [43].[2] EHAP is now entering its most intensive analytical stage; program operations have recently been completed at 10 of the 12 sites (see Figure 1).

The development of an experimental allowance program began in 1971, after Congress passed legislation to examine the feasibility of providing direct cash assistance to lower-income families to enable them to obtain adequate housing at a reasonable cost. As defined by EHAP, a housing allowance is a monthly payment provided to a family that has been determined to be unable to afford a decent home in a suitable living environment. The allowance amount is determined by family need (family size and income) in

---

[1]In some cases, information drawn from program operations in the Supply Experiment refers to earlier dates, which are noted specifically in the text.

[2]Bracket entries refer to items in the Selected Bibliography.

Figure 1

EXPERIMENTAL SITES - EXPERIMENTAL HOUSING ALLOWANCE PROGRAM

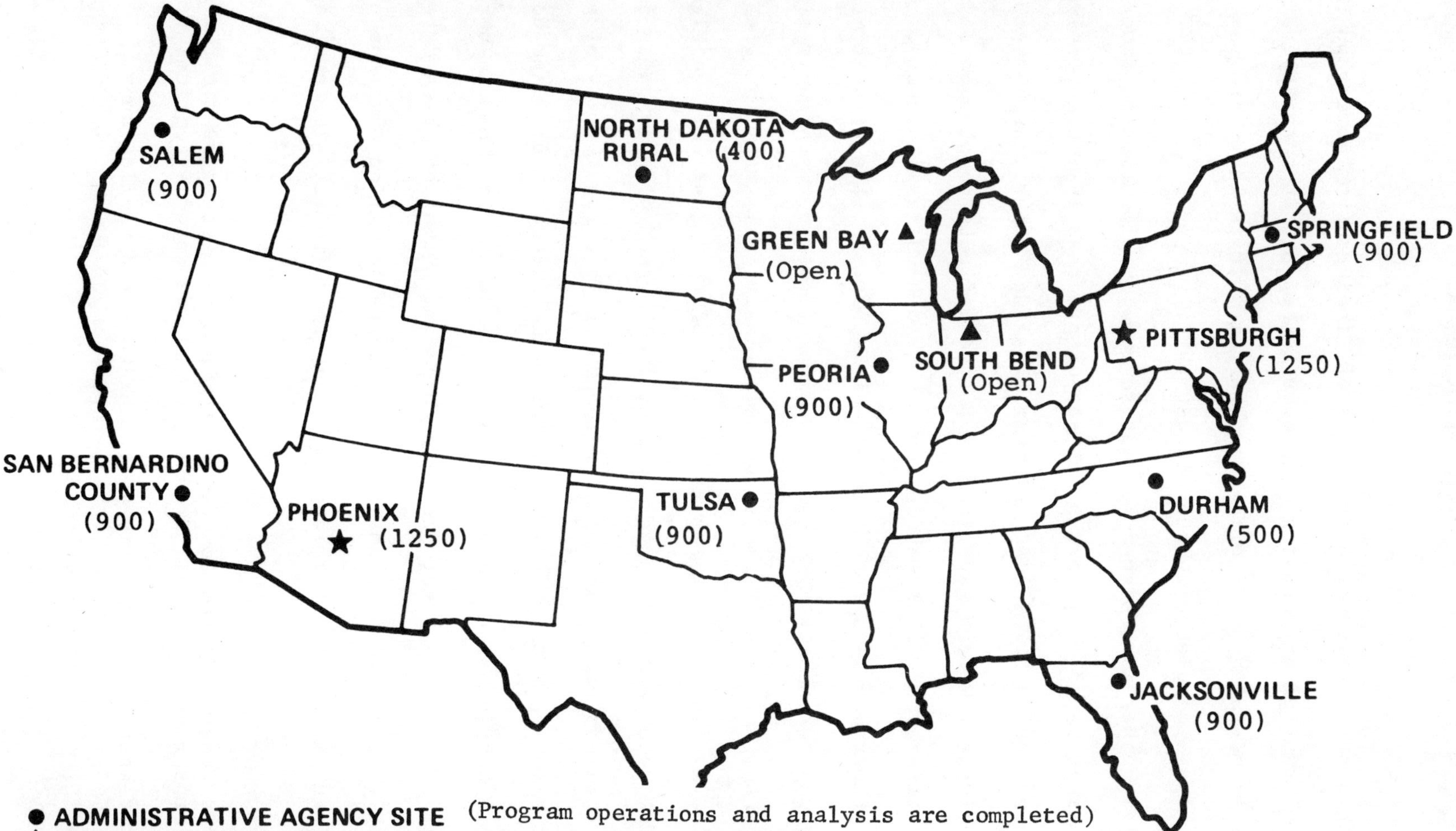

● **ADMINISTRATIVE AGENCY SITE** (Program operations and analysis are completed)
★ **DEMAND EXPERIMENT SITE** (Program operations completed)
▲ **SUPPLY EXPERIMENT SITE** (Program operations continuing)
Planned number of recipient households at each site indicated in parentheses

relation to the cost of standard, existing housing in a modest neighborhood. Unlike most other housing subsidy programs, payments are made directly to participants, who can then choose their housing, as long as they occupy dwellings that meet program housing requirements.[1]

EHAP has not only generated a great deal of information regarding the behavior of allowance recipients, particularly various groups of participating families (e.g., minorities, the elderly), but it has also developed significant insights into the operation of diverse housing markets under the impact of different types of allowance approaches. And it provides much-needed knowledge about the costs and functions of different administrative arrangements for managing an allowance-type program.

EHAP research makes an important contribution to understanding how public interventions affect participants and the housing conditions prevalent in urban and non-metropolitan neighborhoods. It also provides timely insight into how variations of a housing allowance might be used as one aspect of a restructured national welfare system.

An earlier EHAP report completed in February 1976 addressed issues of feasibility and also described some previous findings, based upon 2.5 years of operation [4, 63]. It is now possible to view these findings with the benefit of an additional two years of program experience and completed analysis.

Some statements that appear in this report are based upon early stages of program experience. The results presented here and in other EHAP research documents (see the Selected Bibliography) will be clarified and strengthened

---

[1]See Appendix A for a more detailed discussion of the EHAP housing allowance concept and program design.

as the full analysis is reported in the future. It is important to note that all the analysis in this paper is limited to evidence from EHAP's 12 sites with the exception of Section V, where transfer costs are extrapolated to a national level.[1] The findings stated in qualitative terms are based on careful interpretation of the evidence that reflects reasoned judgments; the quantitative findings presented can typically be interpreted as statistically significant.

Although there are many common aspects to all three experiments, there is no single housing allowance program being tested in this research. Important program differences exist across the experiments and among the sites of the Administrative Agency Experiment, particularly in outreach and enrollment procedures, program housing requirements and services provided to participants. While these differences add richness to the analysis, they must be carefully controlled in interpreting the results.

It should be emphasized that EHAP is a research effort, not an ongoing, operational program. It is designed specifically to understand how certain households respond to the program, as well as to observe institutional and housing market behavior. As a far-ranging social experiment, EHAP's basic purpose is to provide much-needed information to concerned policy makers, so that informed decisions can be made regarding the future of housing programs.

---

[1]The sites were selected through somewhat different processes in each of the three experiments; a comparison of their characteristics with those of the nation's urbanized areas indicates that they mirror reasonably well averages and distributions on variables considered important in analyzing household responses to housing allowances [68].

Chapter II.

PARTICIPATION IN HOUSING ALLOWANCE PROGRAMS

One of the primary objectives of EHAP is to identify which households among the eligible population are able and willing to participate in the experiment and to extrapolate that experience to a large-scale, open-enrollment program. The experimental program therefore seeks to develop an understanding of overall rates of participation, as well as differential levels of participation for various types of lower-income households (e.g., the elderly or the working poor).

In EHAP, households are defined as participants if they have applied for enrollment, met all program requirements (especially income and housing quality standards) and thereby receive allowance payments. The size and composition of the participant population is important for three reasons. First, the rate of participation (i.e., the rate at which eligible families become allowance recipients) directly affects program costs. Second, the degree to which different types of low-income households are active in the experiments is extremely important to an understanding of how housing programs can assist these different groups. If some groups are more reluctant than others to enroll in housing programs, or if some types of families have more difficulty in finding units that meet program standards, there could be an inequitable distribution of program benefits throughout the low-income eligible population. The experimental design of EHAP provides a variety of experience that helps determine how these differential participation rates are generated--through the interaction of forces, both external and internal to the program--and how certain administrative procedures may result in a more equitable distribution of benefits. Third, there is a critical link between the level of participation and public concern to remedy the deterioration of neighborhoods and the housing stock. Low-income households often are unable to afford the expenditures that will maintain their housing, and landlords renting to such households feel that they will not recapture the costs of repairs. But housing assistance can provide a solution in this regard only to the extent that there is participation by sufficiently large numbers of families to change income patterns throughout entire neighborhoods.

The Process of Becoming a Participant

This process involves two basic steps: enrollment and becoming an allowance recipient. Enrollment includes various outreach methods to inform eligible households of the program and to encourage them to enroll, followed by a check to ensure that households meet all program income, tenure and household composition requirements. To become an allowance recipient, a household must reside in a unit that meets program housing requirements.

Enrollment policies and procedures differed significantly among the three elements of EHAP. Agencies in the Administrative Agency Experiment were limited in the total number of recipients that would be permitted, and they were encouraged to enroll different types of families (e.g., elderly or minority households) so that the resultant mix would approximate the composition of the eligible population. To accomplish this, each agency placed certain controls on the enrollment process, including the methods and intensity of outreach [12].

In contrast to the enrollment process in the Administrative Agency Experiment sites, which was established to test various administrative procedures, the Supply and Demand Experiments were designed to gain a broader understanding of participation rates themselves. In the Supply Experiment, enrollment is open to all eligible households (both renters and homeowners) over a ten-year period. The program has had continuous, widespread publicity, although the application process must be initiated by individual households. In the two Demand sites, a sample of households was individually contacted, following surveys, and given a more extensive explanation of the program than is true of typical approaches to enrolling households.

Patterns of Enrollment

Because enrollment procedures varied among the three experiments, it is not surprising that enrollment outcomes also differed (see Table 1). The 22-percent median site enrollment rate for the Administrative Agency Experiment has little comparability to the rates for the other experiments because of the limits placed upon the numbers of recipients at each site. In Pittsburgh, by contrast, 55 percent of the estimated eligible (renter) households were enrolled, and in Phoenix the figure was 60 percent. In the two Supply sites, estimated enrollment rates as of August 1977 were about 60 percent for renters and about 30 percent for homeowners. Enrollment is still open in these two sites, but program operations appear to have reached steady-state conditions.

The enrollment rates in the Demand sites reflect that experiment's objective of developing a controlled sample that was statistically representative of the overall eligible population. It also was a result of the personalized outreach methods used to inform potential enrollees of the program--the only sites where this was done. It is unlikely that these outreach procedures would be repeated in a large-scale, national allowance program. However, the enrollment experience of renters in the Supply Experiment is similar to that of the Demand Experiment, where enrollment was limited to renters. (See Table 1).

Table 1

ENROLLMENT RATES AT THE TWELVE EHAP SITES

Experiment/Site	Specific Experiment Features	Estimated Number of Eligible Households[a]	Number of Households Enrolled	Enrollment Rate (percent)
Administrative Agency Experiment				
Bismarck	Limited publicity, participant-initiated applications, ceiling on number of recipients, limited enrollment period, renters only	2,176	569	26
Durham		5,620	1,231	22
Jacksonville		17,429	1,696	10
Peoria		5,235	2,064	39
Salem		5,232	2,434	47
San Bernardino		19,745	1,926	10
Springfield		17,572	2,334	13
Tulsa		8,734	1,850	21
Median of sites				22
Demand Experiment				
Phoenix	Individually contacted households, one-time enrollment offer, renters only	605[c]	366	60
Pittsburgh		633	351	55
Supply Experiment				
Renters	Continuous publicity, participant-initiated applications, open enrollment, renters and homeowners			
Green Bay		3,760	2,293[d]	61
South Bend		4,645	2,875	62
Homeowners				
Green Bay		4,203	1,342	32
South Bend		10,935	3,384	31

[a]Estimates of the eligible population upon which these enrollment rates are based were made using experimental data from the Demand and Supply Experiments as of the date when the program began at each site. In the Administrative Agency Experiment, no such procedure was possible. Therefore, the eligible population is based on 1970 Census data; these figures are roughly approximate estimates of eligibility.

[b]The entries for the Administrative Agency Experiment indicate eligible households that applied for enrollment. Not all these families were eventually enrolled because a ceiling on the number of recipients required agencies to select a smaller number of households.

[c]These households were contacted for enrollment after their eligibility was estimated through a two-stage survey process. The entries are for only those households offered allowance programs with a housing gap payment formula similar to that used in all EHAP sites (housing gap plans 1 through 9 as listed in Appendix A, Table A-2). For analytic purposes, households are excluded with incomes above the eligibility income used for plans 3, 6 and 9. The Demand Experiment also included additional households that were offered different forms of housing allowance programs.

[d]The entries are based on the number of households enrolled as of August 12, 1977 (38 months of open-enrollment in Green Bay and 28.5 months in South Bend).

The most policy-relevant enrollment experience for an open-enrollment program is that of the two Supply sites, where the program is available to all eligible renters and homeowners, with no restrictive time constraints on the enrollment period. Outreach has been primarily through the media and direct mail.

Looking at the overall enrollment process in EHAP's 12 sites, the most important factors affecting enrollment patterns are

- Program awareness--The evidence is quite clear throughout EHAP that more intensive outreach programs (increased use of the media, etc.) can raise enrollment levels. It also appears that by targeting outreach to special groups of eligible families (e.g., the elderly and the working poor), reluctance to enroll can be overcome to some extent.
- "Welfare stigma"--Eligible families, who are unfamiliar with income-conditioned transfer programs (e.g., Aid to Families with Dependent Children), appear more reluctant to enroll than families that are familiar with such programs. There is some evidence that one reason for this hesitance is a perceived "welfare stigma" attached to programs such as housing allowances. This appears to vary by different groups (e.g., it is stronger for the working poor than for families familiar with welfare) and by different sites. It has been demonstrated that outreach methods can assist in raising the enrollment rates for these families.

- Payment levels--Eligible families, both in the Demand and the Supply Experiments, were less likely to enroll if they were scheduled to receive smaller payments [31, 43]. These lower allowances would typically be paid to households with higher incomes--those whose incomes are closer to the cutoff level set for program eligibility.

The factors cited above affected different groups of eligible households in different ways. Although continuing analysis is being carried out to explain more fully the differential rates of enrollment among various groups (see Table 2), the general patterns observed thus far in EHAP are as follows:

- Minority families generally enrolled at higher rates than non-minority families. Evidence from the Administrative Agency Experiment and Demand Experiment sites indicates that black families in particular generally lived in housing of poorer physical quality and were less satisfied with their dwellings and neighborhoods [8, 25]. Many of these families appear to have enrolled in order to change these conditions.
- Homeowners enrolled at much lower rates than renters. Some eligible homeowners may have avoided the program because they thought their homes could not pass housing quality standards tests; others may have thought that the program was only for renters, and did not enroll for that reason.
- The elderly enrolled at generally lower rates than other households. They were usually less aware of the program,

Table 2

ENROLLMENT RATES IN THE THREE EHAP EXPERIMENTS,
BY HOUSEHOLD CHARACTERISTICS
(Percent of eligible households)

	Renters			Homeowners
Household Characteristics	Administrative Agency Experiment (Limited Enrollment)	Demand Experiment[a]	Supply Experiment[b]	Supply Experiment[b]
Population Group[c]				
Elderly	6	43	39	23
Welfare	70	77	72	29
Working poor	10	54	50	35
Sex of Head				
Male	13	53	38	20
Female	21	61	68	36
Race/Ethnicity				
Minority	26	62	74	46
Non-minority	14	56	49	25
TOTAL	17	58	54	27

NOTE: Estimates of the eligible population upon which these enrollment rates are based were made using experimental data from the Demand and Supply Experiments as of the date when the program began at each site. In the Administrative Agency Experiment, no such procedure was possible. Therefore, the eligible population is based on 1970 Census data, although they were not sufficiently detailed to allow precise determination of eligibility. In particular, the enrollment rate for welfare households is probably overestimated and the rate for working poor underestimated.

[a]These households were contacted for enrollment after their eligibility was estimated through a two-stage survey process. The entries are for only those households offered allowance programs with a housing gap formula similar to that used in all EHAP sites (housing gap plans 1 through 9 listed in Appendix A, Table A-2). For analytic purposes, households are also excluded with incomes above the eligibility income used for plans 3, 6 and 9. The Demand Experiment also included additional households that were offered different forms of housing allowance programs.

[b]The entries are based on the number of households enrolled as of June 1976 in Green Bay (24 months of open enrollment) and December 1976 in South Bend (21.5 months). Entries for minority renters and homeowners and for welfare homeowners reflect fewer than 200 households enrolled in each category in Green Bay.

[c]Households are characterized as elderly if the head is 65 years of age or older; welfare, if they receive any income from welfare and are non-elderly; working poor, if they are neither elderly nor welfare households.

[d]Households that are headed by a black, Spanish-American, Oriental or Native-American individual.

and in the Administrative Agency Experiment sites applied at lower rates than did others [17].

- The working poor appeared to be more reluctant than welfare households to enroll in the program, and this could stem from their unfamiliarity with welfare-type programs in general.
- Female-headed families enrolled at higher rates than male-headed families.

Meeting Program Housing Requirements--Housing Quality Standards and Minimum Rent

Before an enrolled household can receive allowance payments, it must live in a unit that meets program requirements--housing quality standards or minimum rent requirements. Housing quality standards which were used for all households in the Administrative Agency and Supply Experiments and some households in the Demand Experiment are based upon widely understood measures of the physical attributes of a housing unit [16, 67]: condition of walls and ceilings; amount of light, heat and ventilation; overcrowding (persons per room, per bedroom or per square foot), etc. Minimum rent requirements, which were used only for some households in the Demand Experiment, were designed to test the assumption that rent level and housing quality correspond, and established required rent levels as percentages (either 70 or 90 percent) of the estimated cost of modest but adequate housing (see Appendix A). Throughout EHAP, both the specific elements included in the various housing standards and how those standards are implemented differed across the experiments and across the sites of the Administrative Agency Experiment. Understanding these differences and their effects is crucial to an understanding of EHAP results.

A special study undertaken as part of the Integrated Analysis of EHAP indicates that program housing standards and their application are important factors in explaining participation rate differences between the Demand and the Supply Experiments [67]. Although it was found that actual physical conditions of a sample of rental units inspected by professionals from both experiments showed no significant difference between the Demand and Supply sites, approximately 75 percent of the jointly evaluated units failed to meet the Demand Experiment's standards, either because of their physical condition or their size in relation to the number of members in the family; 60 percent failed the Supply Experiment's standards. Approximately 70 percent of the units in the Demand Experiment failed because of physical conditions alone; the figure for the Supply Experiment was 55 percent.

Achieving Allowance Recipient Status

The rate at which enrolled households became recipients varied considerably among sites and experiments. Cross-experimental comparison indicates that the highest rates occurred in three of the Administrative Agency Experiment sites (see Table 3), where over 85 percent of all households enrolled became recipients. The percentage of enrolled families that achieved recipient status in the two Demand sites was significantly lower than in the two other experiments. During the first year, the average rate in the Demand Experiment for those who were required to meet housing quality standards was 43 percent. As noted, one important reason for this lower rate appears to be the relatively high housing standards used in the Demand sites, as compared with those of the Supply Experiment.

Different groups of enrollees became recipients at different rates in the EHAP sites. As in the enrollment process, there were a number of factors at work making it more or less difficult for the various groups to become allowance recipients. The most important of these has already been discussed in the previous section: housing requirements and their application.

Table 3

OVERALL RATES OF EHAP ENROLLEES THAT ACHIEVED RECIPIENT STATUS IN ALLOWANCE PROGRAMS WITH HOUSING QUALITY STANDARDS
(Percent)

Experiment/Site	Renters	Homeowners
Administrative Agency[a]		
Bismarck	86	--
Durham	71	--
Jacksonville[b]	33	--
Peoria	65	--
Salem	86	--
San Bernardino	82	--
Springfield	70	--
Tulsa	86	--
Total Administrative Agency	71	--
Demand[c]		
Phoenix	51 (55)[d]	--
Pittsburgh	36 (53)	--
Total Demand	43 (54)	--
Supply[e]		
Green Bay	80	85
South Bend	65	85
Total Supply	72	85

NOTE: Rates of achieving recipient status are defined as the ratio of households who ever qualified for at least one allowance payment to households who ever enrolled. In the Demand Experiment, figures reflect only those households who received a payment during one year after enrollment and those enrollees who remained eligible for allowances at the end of one year.

[a]Enrolled households typically had no more than 90 days in which to find housing that met housing quality standards in this experiment.

[b]Figures refer to the first enrollment period only.

[c]The entries are for only those households enrolled in allowance programs with a housing gap payment formula, with housing quality standards, and with the same rate at which the allowance is reduced as income increases as is used in the other experiments (plans 1 through 3 as defined in Appendix A, Table A-2). For analytic purposes, households are also excluded with incomes above the eligibility income used for plan 3. The Demand Experiment also included additional households that received different forms of housing allowance payments.

[d]The entries in parentheses are for households defined in (c) above, except housing gap plans 1 through 9, rather than 1 through 3 only, are included.

[e]Entries are based on 38 months of open enrollment in Green Bay and 28.5 months in South Bend as of August 12, 1977.

A dashed entry indicates not applicable.

It appears that the requirements were the major stumbling block for families trying to achieve recipient status. Demand Experiment results provide evidence that participation under a housing quality standards requirement would be lower than under a minimum rent requirement that would result in approximately the same average level of housing expenditures for participants [31].

The experience of the Demand Experiment also suggests that housing requirements have a stronger effect on the chances of achieving recipient status for lower-income families and larger families within the enrolled population. Those households were less likely to have met housing requirements at enrollment and, because of this, subsequently were less likely to meet them [31].

Besides housing requirements, there were other factors that were important contributors to the patterns of achieving recipient status:

- Site housing conditions--The condition of housing at the sites is associated with rates at which enrollees became participants. This was demonstrated most vividly in the two Supply sites, where uniform housing standards were applied to units in both Green Bay and South Bend [43]. The overall failure rate for pre-enrollment dwellings for renters and homeowners in Green Bay (through September 1976) was 49 percent, compared to a 56-percent rate in South Bend. In addition, units in South Bend averaged more critical defects causing failures. This reflects the generally poorer condition of South Bend's housing stock.
- Site mobility rates [64]--The effect of this factor showed up most clearly in the contrast between Phoenix and Pittsburgh, the two Demand sites. At enrollment, a higher percentage of Pittsburgh enrollees met the housing requirements than in Phoenix [27, 31].

After one year of program experience, the percentage of enrollees meeting housing requirements (both quality standards and minimum rent) and participating at the two sites was about the same (see Table 3). The elimination of this difference appears to be attributable to the higher propensity of families in Phoenix to move [27]. Moving increased the likelihood from 2 to 2.5 times that enrolled households not meeting housing requirements at enrollment would become recipients.

- Tight housing markets and segregated residential patterns--These factors influenced achievement of recipient status. An extreme example is Jacksonville in the Administrative Agency Experiment, where the low vacancy rate for inner-city rental housing and a segmented market for lower-rent housing was combined with two other elements previously mentioned--low-quality units and strict housing standards--to produce relatively low rates of households that achieved recipient status, particularly among blacks [10, 11].

These elements, often working in combination, affected different groups in different ways. In particular, minority households had generally less success in becoming recipients in all experiments (see Table 4). Minority families generally had to do more to achieve recipient status--their housing conditions at enrollment were generally worse than non-minority families, and so more minorities found it necessary to move or upgrade their units in order to receive payments.

Table 4

ENROLLEES THAT ACHIEVED RECIPIENT STATUS, BY HOUSEHOLD CHARACTERISTICS (Percent)

Household Characteristics	Renters			Homeowners
	Administrative Agency Experiment[a]	Demand Experiment[b]	Supply Experiment[c]	Supply Experiment[c]
Population Group[d]				
Elderly	78	35	80	88
Welfare	70	52	70	76
Working poor	69	58	68	80
Sex of Head				
Male	73	51	67	81
Female	70	50	73	84
Race/Ethnicity				
Minority[d]	58	43	62	76
Non-minority	77	54	73	84
TOTAL	71	50	71	83

[a]Enrolled households typically had no more than 90 days in which to find housing that met housing quality standards in this experiment.

[b]The entries are for only those households enrolled in allowance programs with a housing gap payment formula similar to that used in all EHAP sites (housing gap plans 1 through 9 listed in Appendix A, Table A-2). For analytic purposes, households are also excluded with incomes above the eligibility income used for plans 3, 6 and 9. The Demand Experiment also included additional households that received different forms of allowance payments.

[c]The entries are based on the ratio of households who ever qualified for at least one allowance payment to households who ever enrolled as of June 1976 in Green Bay (24 months of open enrollment) and December 1976 in South Bend (21.5 months).

[d]Households are characterized as elderly if the head is 65 years or more; welfare, if they receive any income from welfare and are non-elderly; and working poor, if they are neither elderly nor welfare households.

[e]Households that are headed by a black, Spanish-American, Oriental or Native-American individual.

Elderly families and homeowners, on the other hand, had relatively high rates of achieving recipient status once enrolled but many members of these two groups chose not to enroll, perhaps partly because they thought they would have a difficult time qualifying. (The only exception was in the Demand sites, where the enrollment process for the elderly did not tend to produce this pre-enrollment decision.) Neither group has much propensity to move, so if they did not believe their pre-enrollment unit would qualify, they simply chose not to enroll in the program. These patterns are shown in Table 4.

Analysis is continuing to define more precisely the many forces at work in enrolling and becoming a recipient, and to ascertain which are more important to certain types of families. For reasons of equity and program effectiveness, it is important to understand why and how certain low-income groups are affected by these forces, and how methods of outreach, services, and specification and enforcement of program housing requirements influence outcomes.

Chapter III.

HOW PARTICIPANTS ARE ASSISTED BY HOUSING ALLOWANCE PROGRAMS

A fundamental reason to test the housing allowance concept is to observe how the housing situations of low-income families are changed as a result of participation in allowance programs. The housing circumstances of participants were changed in different ways by allowance payments, depending primarily upon whether or not required housing quality standards (or minimum rent) were met at enrollment.

Recipients that Met Program Housing Requirements at Enrollment

Throughout the EHAP experiments to date, about one-half of all recipient families met program housing requirements in the dwellings that they occupied at enrollment without any improvements to the units (see Figure 2). This meant they could receive allowance payments without either moving or upgrading their housing. Analysis of this group of recipients in the Demand Experiment shows that they spent this money as they would have any other income [27]. There were only slight increases in rent after one year of participation (averaging about 2 percent) that could be attributed to the EHAP payments[1] (see Table 5).

---

[1] In addition to the EHAP allowance plans that have program housing requirements, several percent of rent programs were tested in the Demand Experiment. These programs calculated subsidies to households as a fixed percentage of the rent they paid. This type of allowance plan might be expected to lead to increased housing consumption by providing what amounts to a housing price subsidy to the recipient. The first-year findings indicate that the percent of rent subsidies were directly responsible for increased housing expenditures by recipients at both sites--from 2 to 8 percent in Pittsburgh and from 4 to 16 percent in Phoenix, depending on the payment formula used. This approach to the design of a housing allowance program shows promise and will be fully reflected in final EHAP analysis. The percent of rent plans are described in more detail in Appendix A. For the first-year analysis, see [26] in the Selected Bibliography.

Figure 2

MEETING HOUSING REQUIREMENTS:

RECIPIENTS QUALIFYING IN THE THREE EHAP EXPERIMENTS

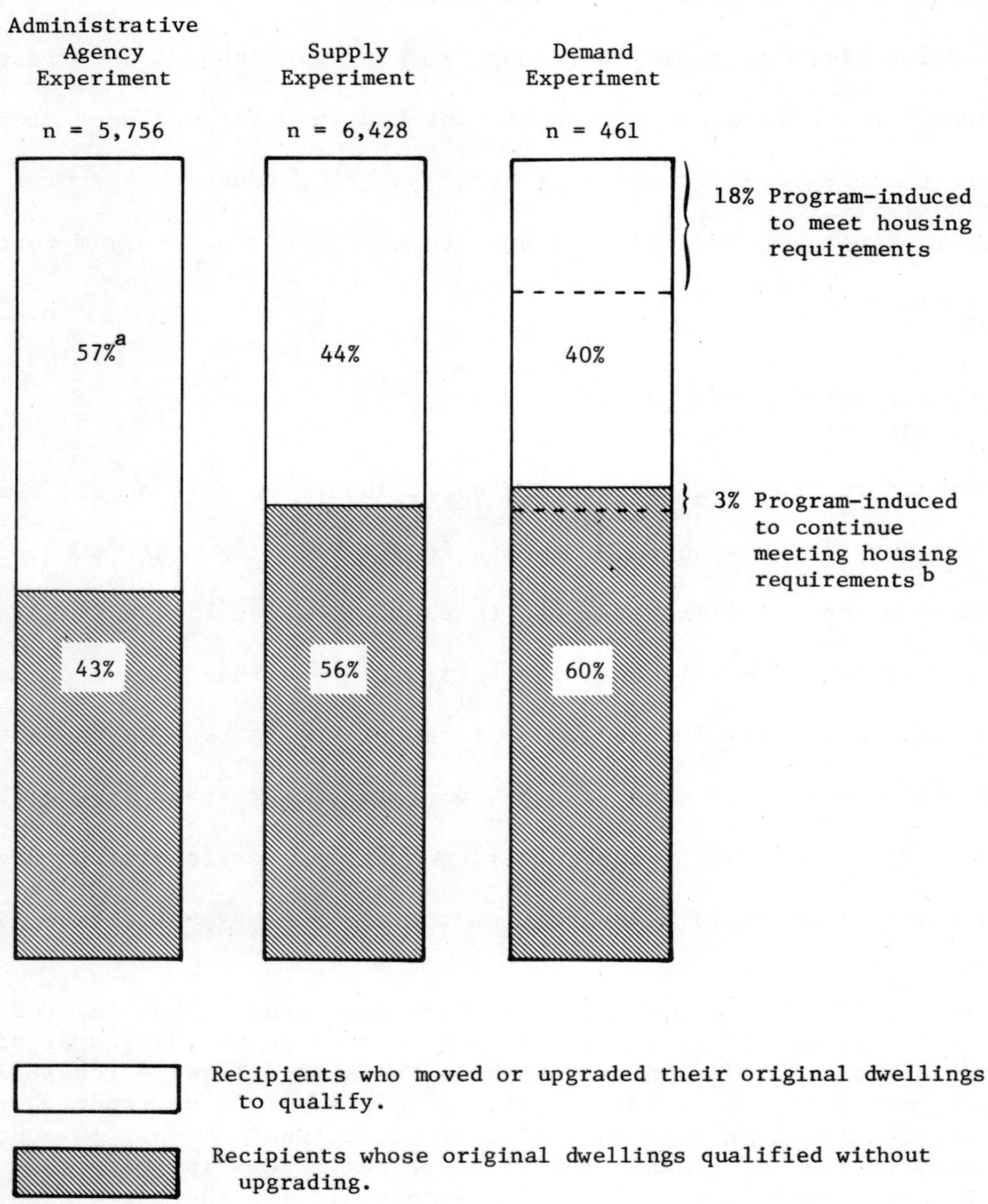

[a]An undetermined number of the Administrative Agency Experiment recipients elected to move even though they could have received payments in their original dwellings.

[b]This program-induced figure is not statistically significant.

Table 5

ESTIMATES OF PROGRAM-INDUCED PERCENTAGE INCREASE IN RENT IN THE DEMAND EXPERIMENT ONE YEAR AFTER ENROLLMENT

All Households and Households that Moved	Percentage Increase in Rent[a]		
	No Housing Requirements[b]	Housing Requirements[c]	
		Met at Enrollment	Met after Enrollment
All Households			
Pittsburgh	1 (69)	2 (148)	12 (90)
Phoenix	7 (46)	2 (104)	26 (106)
Households that Moved			
Pittsburgh	6 (19)	1 (34)	16 (40)
Phoenix	13 (25)	1 (37)	30 (84)

[a]The entries in parentheses refer to numbers of recipients that received allowance payments one year after enrollment.

[b]Estimates are for housing gap households in plan 12 as listed in Appendix A, Table A-2.

[c]Estimates are for housing gap households in plans 1 through 11 as listed in Appendix A, Table A-2.

Even though participating families that met program requirements at the time of their enrollment did not increase their spending for housing by very much, there was another effect on their housing conditions that is perceived most clearly in the Supply Experiment. This evidence indicates that some families might have either moved to a substandard unit or let their units fall below program standards if they had not received allowance payments and thereby been required to occupy standard housing. In Green Bay, for instance, 21 percent of the units that passed evaluations initially failed to pass them one year later, but virtually all these units were upgraded, and their tenants (or owners) remained in the program. Experience in South Bend is shorter and, as previously noted, housing quality there is somewhat lower than in Green Bay. About 36 percent of units in South Bend that passed initial evaluations failed a year later, and about one-half of these were brought up to standard [43].

Recipients that Failed To Meet Requirements at Enrollment

For the families whose original dwelling did not meet program housing requirements, the allowance could not be treated simply as an income supplement. These families had to take action to improve their housing circumstances in order to receive payments, either by upgrading their units or by moving to units that met program requirements (physical standards or a higher rent).

It was the program requirements that induced these families to make substantial improvements in their housing conditions. This is a fundamental distinction between a housing allowance and other, unrestricted forms of cash transfers--allowances as tested in the Demand Experiment have the effect of inducing a greater improvement in housing conditions for recipients that do not meet requirements at enrollment. (See Table 5 for a comparison of program-induced rent increases for this group and for a group of households included in the Demand Experiment design who received equivalent allowances but faced no housing requirements. These households provide a basis for estimating the incremental effect of the housing requirements.)

However, a trade-off exists between the effects of program housing requirements on the housing circumstances of participants and the effects of requirements on how families participate, as discussed in Section II. The existence and stringency of program housing requirements have a positive influence on the housing expenditure patterns of some participants, but they also have a negative effect on the number of eligible families who are willing and able to participate.

Improvements in housing conditions for allowance recipients have been analyzed to date in two ways: (1) increases in housing expenditures, particularly increases associated with families that moved and (2) improvements in recipients' dwelling units associated with meeting program housing requirements.

Increases in Housing Expenditures

The Demand Experiment is the only component of EHAP where, through use of a control group, analysis to date has isolated program-induced effects from other factors that could have affected rent increases. For the two Demand sites, rent increases attributable to the effect of the first year of the allowance program averaged about 20 percent for those recipients who had not met program housing requirements initially (see Table 5). This rent increase absorbed about one-half of their allowance payments [27]. Although differing by site, it is clear that most of this increase is associated with families who moved. In Pittsburgh, families that met housing requirements only after moving were paying rents 16 percent higher that can be attributed to the allowance program. In Phoenix, the equivalent figure was 30 percent. Because the proportion of allowance participants who move can be expected to increase over time, the magnitude of rent increases that movers experience should be given greater weight in developing longer-run estimates of allowance impacts. It will be important in future analytic work to take account of this.

It is instructive to compare rent increases for recipients in the Administrative Agency and Supply Experiments to those in the Demand Experiment in programs with housing quality standards, even though this can only be done at present for changes in gross rents for movers and non-movers (see Table 6). In the Administrative Agency Experiment sites, a somewhat greater percentage

Table 6

MOBILITY AND GROSS RENT INCREASES OF EHAP RENTER RECIPIENTS IN PROGRAMS WITH HOUSING QUALITY STANDARDS

Experiment/Site	Number of Recipients	Changes from Enrollment to Post-Enrollment[a]					
		Movers			Non-Movers		
		Percent of Site Recipients	Average Rent at Enrollment	Percentage Rent Increase	Percent of Site Recipients	Average Rent at Enrollment	Percentage Rent Increase
Administrative Agency Experiment							
Bismarck	407	19	$ 99	48	81	$ 121	3
Durham	430	38	102	45	62	120	2
Jacksonville[b]	270	58	100	76	42	138	8
Peoria	791	30	109	46	70	125	1
Salem	847	48	112	44	52	136	1
San Bernardino	775	44	119	42	56	133	2
Springfield	800	42	130	40	58	144	3
Tulsa	841	40	107	47	60	127	2
Total Administrative Agency	5,161	40	113	45	60	130	2
Demand Experiment[c]							
Pittsburgh	78	29	108	42	71	121	7
Phoenix	91	53	130	39	47	150	6
Total Demand	169	42	113	40	58	139	7
Supply Experiment							
Green Bay	1,598	28	144	32	72	148	10
South Bend	1,679	28[d]	135	34	72	148	5
Total Supply	3,277	28	139	33	72	148	7

[a]Data on post-enrollment reflect time of first payment in the Administrative Agency Experiment (generally no more than three months after enrollment), one year of program participation in the Demand Experiment and approximately two years of program operations in the Supply Experiment (two years in Green Bay, one year and nine months in South Bend). The average period of enrollment for Supply Experiment households is about 11 months.

[b]The entries refer to the first enrollment period only.

[c]These entries are for only those participants required to meet program housing quality standards, housing gap plans 1 through 3, 10 and 11, as listed in Appendix A, Table A-2; they refer to those households that received allowance payments one year after enrollment. The Demand Experiment also included additional households that received different forms of housing allowance payments.

[d]Includes 26 recipients who were living in subsidized housing but subsequently moved to unsubsidized housing to receive allowance payments. Recipients in this category were excluded from the figures in the other experiments.

of families moved (considering the differences in time periods between the experiments over which moves were measured, as noted in the table), and the percentage rent increases for movers were also somewhat greater than in the Demand Experiment sites. In the Supply Experiment, there has been much less mobility observed to date for renters, and the gross rent increases for movers have been smaller than those observed in the Demand Experiment. It should be noted, however, that there is a great difference in mobility behavior between the two Demand sites. The Pittsburgh experience is more aligned with the Supply results; Phoenix is more like the Administrative Agency Experiment. Work is continuing in the Integrated Analysis to explain these cross-experimental and cross-site differences in behavior and to permit better isolation of program-induced effects in the Administrative Agency and Supply Experiments.

Improvements in Dwelling Units Associated with Requirements

A second way in which improvements in housing conditions have been analyzed to date is by measuring the improvements in recipient dwelling units attributable to program housing requirements. The Supply Experiment permits measures of changes associated with housing units that originally failed program housing standards but were subsequently brought into compliance. For the period from January 1976 through June 1977, the median "out-of-pocket" cost per dwelling unit for repairs to bring those dwellings up to standard was $10 per unit, although most of the labor was supplied by the tenant or the landlord/owner (see Table 7). These costs are based on 1,595 units repaired in Green Bay and 3,505 in South Bend in response to failed-unit evaluations. Two categories of repairs accounted for about half of the total in both sites: handrail repaired, replaced or installed; and

Table 7

CASH EXPENDITURES FOR INITIAL REPAIRS TO PARTICIPANTS' DWELLING UNITS: SUPPLY EXPERIMENT, BY SITE, 1976-1977

Cash Expenditures per Dwelling Unit ($)	Percentage Distribution of Dwellings Repaired			
	Green Bay		South Bend	
	Renters	Homeowners	Renters	Homeowners
Repaired with no cash expenditure	25.3	17.3	24.4	21.4
Repaired, by amount of expenditure				
$ 1 - 20	49.3	55.2	42.8	46.2
21 - 40	10.2	10.2	15.3	13.8
41 - 100	9.5	10.8	12.8	9.7
101 - 200	2.8	3.1	2.5	3.5
201 or more	2.9	3.2	2.2	5.3
Median cost ($)	8	10	10	11
Average cost ($)	39	55	37	81

NOTE: Costs were estimated by participants and do not include unpaid labor. Renters may lack information on costs paid by landlords. Percentages may not add to 100 due to rounding.

windows opened, repaired, replaced or installed. Overall, about one-third of all units occupied by recipients in the Supply Experiment have undergone some form of upgrading, largely modest improvements. More extensive repairs have, however, been reported for some units [43].

In the Demand Experiment, an attempt was made to determine the percentage of recipients induced by the program during their first year of involvement to live in standard housing (or housing that met mimimum rent requirements) that otherwise would have not met program housing requirements. After removing other factors, less than one-half of those families that had not met program requirements initially and met them a year later (18 percent of total recipients) were estimated to have been induced to meet them by the allowance program (see Figure 2).

Other Evidence of Program Impact

Three additional areas have been considered in the analysis to date of how low-income families are affected by housing allowances: mobility, neighborhood quality, and racial concentration; overcrowding; and reduction of housing costs relative to income.

Mobility, Neighborhood Quality, and Racial Concentration. Current EHAP evidence indicates that housing allowances have not influenced families to move any more often than they would have ordinarily [69]. This is seen most clearly in the Demand Experiment, where the mobility of allowance recipients has been compared to a control group that did not receive allowance payments. There has not been any significant difference between mobility rates of experimental and control households to date [29]. Preliminary analysis of data from the other two experiments generally supports this conclusion, although there is evidence which suggests that mobility may have been affected by the program at several Administrative Agency Experiment sites [69].

In addition to possible effects on mobility rates, it is important to understand where participants moved and whether or not they moved to neighborhoods of better quality. It should be noted that housing allowance programs tested in EHAP could result only indirectly in neighborhood quality changes. Program features provide no direct incentive for neighborhood improvements by recipients; housing quality standards do not include any neighborhood characteristics.

Neighborhood quality is difficult to measure. In the Demand Experiment, concentration of low-income households in census tracts has been used as a proxy measure of neighborhood quality. Low-income concentration is defined by the percentage of households in a census tract with incomes under $5000, as reported in the 1970 Census. In addition to the low-income concentration index, household locations in the Demand Experiment have been characterized by participants' perceptions of neighborhood quality elicited through responses to a number of survey questions [30].

Neither the low-income concentration index nor participants' evaluations of neighborhoods indicates allowance-induced improvements in neighborhood quality among families who moved during the first year of the Demand Experiment. Experimental households--defined for this analysis as those who were offered an allowance--who moved did improve their neighborhood quality somewhat according to these measures, but changes for control household movers were approximately the same.

Analysis to date of neighborhood change in the Administrative Agency Experiment used as an indicator of neighborhood quality an index based on the income, education, and white collar employment of census tract residents [15].

By this measure, about a quarter of all recipients improved their neighborhood quality between enrollment and the time they received their first allowance payment. However, another one-eighth of all recipients moved to tracts with lower measures of socioeconomic status. Focusing only on those recipients who moved prior to the first payment (about 45 percent of all recipients), 49 percent showed an increase in neighborhood quality and 29 percent experienced a decline. These are gross measures of program effect; there is no control group available as in the Demand Experiment.

The racial composition of neighborhoods is clearly also an issue of policy concern. As with neighborhood quality, EHAP's allowance programs were not designed to achieve any particular pattern of change in location by race; any program effects, therefore, would be indirect. Thus far, there is no evidence from EHAP that housing allowances have substantially altered patterns of racial and ethnic settlement, although some marginal effects for black households have been noted. In the first year of the Demand Experiment, non-minority families in both sites and Spanish-American families in Phoenix who were offered a housing allowance and who moved chose neighborhoods with a racial concentration not significantly different from similar control households who moved. Black households chose neighborhoods of slightly lower racial concentration, on average. But due in part to the small number of movers in the first-year data, these changes also showed no statistically significant differences from those of black control households that moved [30]. Analysis of two years of data from the Demand Experiment should provide clearer evidence on this tentative finding.

Among the black households that moved in the Administrative Agency Experiment, the mean percentage minority of the census tract of residence as measured in 1970 dropped from 56 percent at enrollment to 40 percent at the time of receipt of the first allowance payment. Most of the black families that moved, however, went to tracts in or adjacent to predominantly black areas and generally seemed to be following established patterns of black residential mobility at their sites. Non-minority families moved from tracts that were, on average, 94 percent non-minority to those that were 96 percent non-minority [9].

The limited information available from the Supply Experiment on locational patterns of participants is consistent with evidence from the other two experiments. Preliminary analysis of program experience in South Bend through September 1976 shows a small movement out of racially mixed neighborhoods by white families, and some net movement of black families within these racially mixed neighborhoods from tracts predominantly black in 1970 to tracts predominantly white at that time [43]. Again, this seems generally consistent with established patterns of black residential mobility.

Overcrowding. Severe overcrowding has long been recognized as an important aspect of housing deprivation but, as in other areas of program impact, measures have been difficult to develop. Simple measures have been used in EHAP (e.g., persons per bedroom, per room, or per square foot) and data from the Administrative Agency Experiment indicate that 18 percent of recipient families that moved originally lived in units with more than one person per room [9]. As a result of the move to larger units, one-half of these households were no longer crowded, according to this measure.

Larger families (five or more persons) experienced the greatest reductions in crowding, as might be expected. These families in general had more trouble qualifying as allowance recipients than smaller families--partly as a result of the difficulty in locating sufficiently large units--but larger families differed from smaller families in achieving recipient status by only 8 percentage points.

Reduction in Housing Costs Relative to Income. Families enrolled in EHAP, like many low-income families in the nation, paid high percentages of their incomes for rent. In the Administrative Agency Experiment, recipient households paid a median of 42 percent of their gross incomes for rent and utilities prior to enrollment [9]. In the Demand Experiment, pre-allowance rent burdens also averaged over 40 percent at both sites [27].

Housing allowance payments have provided an important supplement to all participating families' incomes and, with the imposition of program requirements, led to substantial improvements in their housing circumstances. In the Administrative Agency Experiment, average monthly subsidy payments constituted about one-third of the pre-payment net income of recipients; in the two Supply sites, the comparable figure was 25 percent as of August 1977.

Chapter IV.
THE EFFECTS OF HOUSING ALLOWANCES ON MARKETS AND COMMUNITIES

The previous section discussed the ways in which housing conditions of allowance recipients are affected by participation in the program, to what extent units are upgraded and how the actions of participants can retard deterioration of the housing stock. This section will examine the ways in which the actions of participants influence housing markets and how local communities respond to the presence of an allowance program.

The possible impact of an allowance program on local housing markets is one of the most critical issues inherent in the allowance approach. If there are significant levels of price inflation (e.g., rent increases that outstrip the increased level of housing services supplied by the market), other potential benefits of an allowance program could be nullified.

Two aspects of EHAP specifically address this issue: (1) the Supply Experiment, currently under way in Green Bay, Wisconsin, and in South Bend, Indiana [43]; and (2) market simulations being carried out as part of the Integrated Analysis, using The Urban Institute's housing market model [65, 66]. These simulations are designed to test the possible effects of allowance programs of varying sizes and types in different sorts of housing markets.

Dimensions of the Supply Experiment

The experiment in Green Bay and South Bend is designed to measure market effects over a five-year period. Some analysis of the first 27 months of the program in Green Bay and the first 18 months in South Bend has been completed. In both sites, the program is offered to all households that meet certain basic income and housing quality standards (except single, non-elderly individuals) to enable evaluation of market-wide impacts.[1] The Supply Experiment is the only element of EHAP that offers open enrollment to all households, including low-income homeowners.

The two market situations in the Supply Experiment are quite different--Green Bay has a tight housing market, with a housing stock of relatively high quality. It grew rapidly during the 1960s. Only 2 percent of the county's residents are members of minority groups. South Bend, by contrast, has a higher vacancy rate for both homeowner and rental units, a county population that is declining, and a black population that is now 18 percent of the central city population. South Bend's housing is generally of poorer quality and household incomes are lower than in Green Bay. In terms of the central city growth rate and its percentage of minorities--in this case, black families--South Bend appears to be similar to SMSAs (Standard Metropolitan Statistical Areas) containing about one-half of the nation's metropolitan population, while Green Bay resembles about one-fourth of the nation's metropolitan population.

In Green Bay, roughly 17 percent of the total households in the county were estimated to be eligible for the program as of September 1976. About 9 percent of all households in the county had been allowance recipients at some point during the program; about 6 percent of all households were receiving allowance payments as of that time. In South Bend, where the program is nine

---

[1]As of August 1, 1977, single-person families with the head of the household between 18 and 62 years of age became eligible to receive allowance payments at the two Supply sites; however, the number of these households that may receive an allowance is limited to 10 percent of the total recipients authorized under the Annual Contributions Contract.

months behind Green Bay's, about 20 percent of all households were estimated to be eligible, and about 5 percent of the total households were receiving payments.

Measuring Market Impacts

As of September 1976, there was no evidence in either Supply site of increases in rents or homeownership costs induced by the allowance program [43]. In the first year and a half of program experience in Green Bay, market-wide rents rose at about a 6-percent annual rate, but nearly all the increase was due to higher costs of fuel and utilities. The available data show, if anything, that the rents of program participants were less affected by inflation than were rents in the market generally. More limited data of the same period show that South Bend, with a higher vacancy rate and more abandoned units than Green Bay, also exhibits no program-caused price effects.

There appear to be two fundamental reasons why there have been no perceived price effects at the two Supply sites. One is that the level of participation has been lower than anticipated. Second, the participants have increased their housing expenditures by only a fraction of the payments they have received. To date, the combined effect of participation and consumption behavior of participants has added less than 1 percent to market-wide housing expenditures in both sites.

It is still too early to say with certainty that there would not be price effects, particularly in some submarkets. Analysis of time lags in rental housing markets has indicated that there are significant delays, usually several years in duration, before changes in income and the quality of services offered have full impact on the behavior of both renters and landlords. It is not yet certain whether such lags are occurring in the two Supply sites, or what the magnitudes of delayed responses might be.

Simulating Market Effects

Predicting price impacts as a result of an allowance program in other housing markets or for program designs different from that specifically tested in the Supply Experiment is still in the early stages. Applications of The Urban Institute's housing market model have indicated that weak demand for low-quality housing in a market in the absence of an allowance program is an important predictor of inflationary response to a simulated housing allowance program. Calibration of the model to the two Supply Experiment sites as part of the Integrated Analysis has indicated that South Bend exhibits this characteristic and would be more likely than Green Bay to experience allowance-induced price increases [65, 66]. In both cases, simulations produced participation rates higher than have been experienced thus far. Since it now appears that participation in both sites is leveling off, it is important that future policy simulations with the model more accurately reflect actual participation behavior.

Community Acceptance of Housing Allowance Programs

Another important issue is whether or not local communities--governments, private businesses, and citizens--accept a housing allowance program. EHAP has enjoyed a high level of acceptance in all communities where it has been widely advertised and publicized [63]. (In Pittsburgh and Phoenix, families were individually contacted and there was no widespread public enrollment campaign.)

When EHAP was initiated and the sites selected, concerns were voiced about possible direct and indirect impacts of the program. Two possible sites for the Supply Experiment were rejected when suburban jurisdictions resisted the program. In South Bend, all suburban jurisdictions originally declined to cooperate with the program but their fears were gradually allayed, and within 18 months they agreed to join the city of South Bend to undertake the experiment [43]. Expressed concerns covered a wide range of issues initially, but it seems apparent that South Bend's segregated city housing market was an element in the debate. As it became more obvious that payments were assisting needy households, and that program-induced locational changes were minor, opposition seems to have lessened. In Green Bay, where there is little racial difference between city and suburban neighborhoods, there has been little dissent. Local governments and community organizations there have been highly supportive of EHAP.

In both South Bend and Green Bay, resources to support housing improvements are available. Community groups have donated labor, and local governments have allocated funds for home improvement loans and housing rehabilitation.

Chapter V.
PROGRAM ADMINISTRATION AND COSTS

Throughout the experimental program, costs have been carefully monitored and are being analyzed to provide understanding of actual costs in each experimental element and at each site, and to permit extrapolation of EHAP experience to a national level. There are two basic elements to housing allowance program costs: (1) transfer costs--or the costs of allowances paid to participating families, and (2) administrative costs--the cost of managing the process of providing those payments, counseling, keeping records, inspecting units, and other administrative tasks.

Local allowance programs at EHAP sites have been administered by existing agencies as well as by private organizations established especially to manage the experiments in Pittsburgh and Phoenix (the Demand sites), and Green Bay and South Bend (the Supply sites). At the eight sites comprising the Administrative Agency Experiment, various state and local agencies managed the program.

While the experiments themselves have generated the basic body of data on actual costs of the program as it has been operated at the 12 sites, the Integrated Analysis has used a transfer program simulation model (TRIM) to estimate the possible costs of operating an allowance program involving open enrollment at a national level.[1] It is important to understand that while this simulation work estimates transfer costs on a national scale, it is based upon an extrapolation of the real costs of the program as they have been measured throughout EHAP.

---

[1]This simulation work is discussed in detail under the heading "Extrapolating Transfer Costs to a National Level" later in this section. See [60] for a complete description of the TRIM work.

Per-Unit Administrative Costs in EHAP

One part of EHAP, the Administrative Agency Experiment, was designed not only to test various methods of managing the program, but also to measure actual administrative costs [13]. While these costs have also been monitored throughout the work at the Demand and Supply Experiment sites, the Administrative Agency Experiment was designed from its inception to generate cost data in a form that facilitates analysis [54]. It provides the fewest problems of separating costs of administration due to the experimental nature of the program from administrative costs related to normal program operations.

In the Administrative Agency Experiment, eight public agencies in different sections of the nation ran limited-scale housing allowance programs for three years, approximately one year for enrollment and two years of maintenance operations. The agencies were encouraged to develop their own management systems, under limited federal guidelines, and therefore a variety of administrative forms evolved.

Actual administrative costs in EHAP have been analyzed in terms of two basic factors: (1) intake costs, or the cost of bringing families into the program, including administrative costs prior to making payments, and (2) maintenance costs associated with continuing the payments to recipients and providing them with other needed services. In the Administrative Agency Experiment, the median intake cost for all sites was $225 per family, while the site median maintenance cost was $205 per family per year (see Table 8).

To establish a more realistic estimate of the program impact of intake costs, these intake figures were amortized over five years--the average length of time that participating families were assumed to stay in the

Table 8

ADMINISTRATIVE COSTS OF THE ADMINISTRATIVE AGENCY EXPERIMENT
(Annual Rate per Household Assisted)

Site	Intake Costs[a]	Maintenance Costs	Total Administrative Costs[b]
Bismarck	$ 215	235	$ 278
Durham	233	231	278
Jacksonville	230	322	368
Peoria	151	171	201
Salem	178	129	165
San Bernardino	246	178	227
Springfield	219	267	311
Tulsa	292	144	202
Median of site costs	$ 225	$ 205	$ 250

[a]Costs adjusted by median site costs of working with families that later dropped out of the program without becoming recipients.

[b]Assumes intake costs amortized over five years. Thus, "Total Administrative Costs" are one-fifth of "Intake Costs," plus "Maintenance Costs."

program. Thus, the amortized annual intake cost is $45 per year for each family. Adding this amount to the $205 per year that it costs to maintain a family in the allowance system, the total management cost in the Administrative Agency Experiment was $250 per year for each participating family, or about $20 per month. This cost included the cost of contacting families and working with them through the early stages of the program process, although these families sometimes dropped out prior to receiving any payments.

Variation in Administrative Costs

The figures cited for total administrative costs in the preceding paragraphs blur wide divergences in costs among the Administrative

Agency Experiment sites. For example, intake costs ranged from a low of $151 in Peoria to $292 per family in Tulsa (see Table 8). A major reason for this variation was the difference in outreach techniques used for contacting families--Tulsa made heavy use of advertising and the media, while Peoria relied principally upon word-of-mouth and other agencies for referral of families. Maintenance costs showed a similar divergence, from a low of $129 in Salem to $322 in Jacksonville, where the figures were particularly skewed because of the relatively small number of participants, which thereby increased per-family maintenance costs.

The costs due to families dropping out prior to becoming allowance recipients is also an important factor in overall program management costs, amounting to about one-third of total intake costs in the Administrative Agency Experiment. Some of these costs result from external conditions beyond an agency's control. For instance, in the Jacksonville experience, much of the cost of families dropping out was the result of a highly segregated market characterized by generally poor-quality housing in the low-rent sector, which made it difficult for many enrollees to become recipients.

From analysis of actual costs in the Administrative Agency Experiment, it is clear that many factors affect management costs. These include: population density and the size of the area served, quality of the area's housing stock, racial and ethnic composition and prevailing wage rates in the region and area.

Administrative costs in the Administrative Agency Experiment were also significantly affected by the choices and intensity of procedures employed for certain major program functions, especially outreach, housing inspections and the provision of services (e.g., counseling, assistance with leases and transportation). Variations in the performance of other functions--certification of income, enrollment and payments operations--did not lead to significant variations in administrative costs.

The range of direct management costs across agencies is shown in terms of those intake and maintenance functions for which costs varied substantially [13]:

	Range
Intake functions	
Outreach (per applicant)	$ 1 - $ 27
Services (per enrollee)	6 - 45
Housing inspections (per enrollee)	2 - 26
Maintenance functions	
Services (per recipient-year)	11 - 85
Housing inspections (per recipient-year)	1 - 15

In some cases, however, lower costs for these functions were associated with less effectiveness in their performance [18]. For example, it has already been indicated that the type and intensity of outreach directly affected levels and patterns of enrollment. The effectiveness of housing inspections was also closely linked to method and to costs. Several agencies in the Administrative Agency Experiment used tenant inspections of units in place of inspections by professionals or staff generalists; these agencies experienced the lowest cost per unit for their inspections. But spot checks indicated that in nearly two-thirds of the inspections performed by tenants of "marginal units"--those units likely to be considered substandard by most experiment agencies--inadequate information was provided by them. In one site, inspectors who followed up tenant inspections failed 20 percent of the units that had been passed by tenants.

Administrative costs may also be influenced by economies of scale associated with running programs that service more families than were observed in the Administrative Agency Experiment experience, and through possible integration of housing allowance functions with other elements of the welfare system, such as is done currently with the federal food stamp program [54].

Variation in Allowance Payments

Variation in allowance payments to families across the EHAP sites can be accounted for largely by (1) different average program-defined incomes of recipients, (2) variation in the levels set in each locality for the costs of adequate housing and (3) the different types of tenure included in each experiment--the Supply Experiment allows homeowner participation, whereas the other two experiments were limited to renters. The average monthly household subsidy paid in the eight Administrative Agency Experiment sites was about $80, but the range was $72 to $89. In the two Demand sites, average payments were $50 per month in Pittsburgh and $78 in Phoenix for households on housing gap plans with a payment formula most equivalent to those used in the other two experiments. And in the two Supply sites, average monthly payments as of August 1977 were $75 in Green Bay and $70 in South Bend.

Extrapolating Transfer Costs to a National Level

Using the actual per-unit transfer costs experienced in EHAP as a stepping off place, the Integrated Analysis has investigated the national-level costs of housing allowances which permit open enrollment--similar to how enrollment has worked at the Supply Experiment sites.[1] These simulations

[1] A housing allowance program operated by the federal government might, of course, be structured very differently, possibly taking the form of a limited-entitlement program such as Section 8 (Housing Assistance Payments Program--Existing Housing). In that case, while program costs might be higher per family assisted, the total program cost could be much lower. See Appendix A for a more detailed discussion of the Section 8 program.

have assumed varying rates of participation, different payment formulas and alternative ways in which an allowance program might fit with other elements of the welfare system. Other key variables considered include such factors as household incomes and housing costs in various housing market areas throughout the country [60].

The specific extrapolation of EHAP experience reported here is based upon seven basic program assumptions: (1) extension of eligibility to homeowners as well as to renters; (2) exclusion of households headed by students and households consisting of non-elderly single persons; (3) an assumed average national cost of adequate housing, which varies by housing market area but averages about $185 per month for a two-bedroom unit; (4) a payment formula that provides recipient families with an amount equal to the cost of adequate, modest housing less 25 percent of their household incomes; (5) an income definition that excludes taxes and work-related expenses, but that counts cash assistance from other federal programs as income; (6) an imputed return on home equity; and (7) no assets test. One of the roles of the Integrated Analysis is to test the sensitivity of estimates of national-level programs to these and other assumptions.

In addition to specific program features, another critical determinant of the costs of a program with open enrollment is the level of participation--what proportion of all those families eligible for support that are able and willing to take advantage of the opportunity. Extrapolation that draws on EHAP experience but adjusts for differences in housing tenure as well as the composition of the national population indicates an "upper bound" estimate of a national participation rate of about 40 percent of all eligible households.[1]

---

[1]This figure is derived primarily from Green Bay, the Supply Experiment site at which participation rates of 30 percent for homeowners and 50 percent for renters appear to have reached a steady-state in program

Last, this estimate assumes no increases in program costs as a result of program-induced inflation.

Based on these assumptions concerning program features, participation experience and lack of market effects on program costs, about 17.5 million households would be income-eligible and about 7.2 million households (2.4 million homeowners and 4.8 million renters) would receive allowances in a national-level program. The average subsidy level would be about $65 per month.

Total payments costs, given these estimates, would be about $5.7 billion annually in 1976 dollars when the program reaches steady-state (Table 9).[1]

Table 9

PROGRAM ESTIMATES FOR A NATIONAL-LEVEL, OPEN-ENROLLMENT HOUSING ALLOWANCE (In 1976 Dollars)

Tenure	Eligible Households (Millions)	Participant Households (Millions)	Annual Subsidy Cost ($ Billions)	Average Monthly Subsidy ($)
Homeowners	8.0	2.4	1.7	56
Renters	9.5	4.8	4.0	69
TOTAL	17.5	7.2	5.7	66

operations. As noted previously, participation rates are influenced by the type and stringency of the program housing requirements imposed. These estimates implicitly assume the program housing standards used in the Supply Experiment and do not apply to the program housing standards tested in the Demand Experiment. Evidence presented earlier (see Section II) indicates that use of the Demand Experiment standards would result in lower participation rates.

[1]If all single-person, non-elderly households were included in this allowance program, an increase of 1.4 million participating households and $1 billion in transfer costs would result.

Extrapolating Administrative Costs to a National Level

Until analysis currently under way in the Integrated Analysis is completed, the best available estimates from which to extrapolate administrative costs to a national level come from experience in the Administrative Agency Experiment. The estimates indicate a per-family monthly administrative cost of $20, including an amortized intake factor. For the estimated 7.2 million households that would participate at a national level, this would indicate an additional $1.7 billion for program administration. This experience reflects small-scale programs at the agency level and the development of an administrative structure separate from other welfare-system programs--approaches that might not be reflected in a national-level program. Based on specific assumptions regarding EHAP evidence to date, however, extrapolating program costs of a national-level housing allowance would indicate a total cost of about $7.4 billion, or about $85 per month for each participating family. These assumptions and extrapolations will, of course, be revised and tested as EHAP analysis continues.

Appendix A.

BACKGROUND AND DESCRIPTION OF THE EXPERIMENTAL HOUSING ALLOWANCE PROGRAM

This appendix outlines the background of the housing allowance concept and describes the integrated program design underlying EHAP.

Background

Housing allowances or "rent certificates" are not new concepts. They have played a role in discussions of housing policies and programs since debates prior to the passage of the Housing Act of 1937. The Taft Subcommittee hearings on postwar housing policy in 1944 and the long discussions leading to adoption of the Housing Act of 1949 all involved position papers and testimony for and against rent certificates. In 1953, the President's Advisory Committee on Government Housing Policies and Programs also discussed the concept at some length in its report, before rejecting the approach in support of the continuation of the public housing program. The committee concluded that rent certificates would be degrading to recipients, that they would not "add to the housing supply," that they would deter participation by private enterprise, that appropriate administration of the program would be organizationally complex and that there would be no feasible way to limit the scale of such a program.

A shift in housing policy in the direction of housing allowances came in the Housing and Urban Development Act of 1965. Two new housing programs came into existence. The first was the rent supplement program, which limited its subsidies to newly constructed or substantially rehabilitated housing, but established the principle of income-related subsidies to residents of privately owned housing units. The amount of these subsidies varied according to household need.

Rent supplements offered recipients a flexibility not permitted by conventional public housing. They were able to continue to occupy their housing units at market rents when their income increased to the point where they were no longer eligible for assistance. In the rent supplement program, however, payments were made to the owners of eligible housing developments and households benefited only when they resided in such developments.

The second program added in 1965 was the Section 23 leased housing program--a program much closer in design to a housing allowance. It enabled local housing authorities to lease modest but adequate privately owned dwellings and then to sublease them to low-income households. The government paid the difference between the full cost of leasing the private unit and the amount (determined by a formula) of what the family could afford. The Section 23 program had the advantage of being able to use existing housing units scattered through a range of neighborhoods.

The Section 23 approach meant that recipients could be provided substantial anonymity and would not be tightly clustered geographically. The local housing authorities, rather than the family, almost always located and selected the housing and negotiated rents and lease provisions with the landlord. A household did not receive its subsidy directly and could not automatically take the subsidy with it when it decided to move to a new housing unit. Furthermore, under the Section 23 program, a family could only receive a subsidy if it lived in a local jurisdiction which approved the use of the program.

The requirements and guidelines of Section 23 were revised in April 1974. Under these "new" Section 23 provisions, the owners of private housing units essentially assumed the managerial role that had previously been performed by local housing authorities. Owners directly leased the unit to a low-income family, then entered into an agreement with the local agency to cover the difference between the contract rent and the rental payment determined by formula for the low-income tenant. The responsibility of the local administering agency was limited to that of certifying tenant eligibility, inspecting the condition of the unit and making the housing assistance payments to owners.

Several months after the revision of Section 23, a new subsidy program for "low-income" and "very low-income" families--the Section 8 program--was enacted. By January 1975, Section 8, which drew heavily upon the features of "new" Section 23, had been completely phased in as a replacement for the short-lived "new" Section 23. Since its implementation, Section 8 has become the government's main housing subsidy program for low-income families.[1]

Initial Research on Housing Allowances. In 1967 and 1968, the President's Committee on Urban Housing, generally known as the Kaiser Committee, devoted special attention to the housing allowance approach. The Committee did not propose immediate adoption of housing allowances in its report to the President, but did recommend prompt initiation of an experiment to test allowances.

During the following two years, preliminary estimates of the costs of a national program were made which indicated that the subsidy cost per household through the allowance approach would be significantly lower than the

---

[1]See the discussion under the heading "EHAP and the Section 8 (Existing Housing) Program: A Comparison of Features" at the end of this appendix for more details of the Section 8 program.

average subsidy cost per unit under other federal housing programs. An analysis dealing with the rent response that would be brought about by an allowance program revealed the need for more extensive modeling and analysis of market effects and for a more rigorous direct test of the housing allowance concept. Analysis during this period suggested that in the long run the response due to a housing allowance would involve a substantial increase in the quantity of housing [71, 72, 73].

Kansas City and Wilmington Demonstrations. At the same time that analysis of the housing allowance concept was taking place, the Kaiser Committee recommendation was translated into action under HUD's Model Cities program. The local Model Cities agencies of two cities, Kansas City, Missouri, and Wilmington, Delaware, began demonstration programs in late 1970 designed to use housing allowances as a means of providing decent housing. An evaluation of both the Kansas City and the Wilmington demonstrations provides some insights into the effects of housing allowances [78].

Conceptual Design of an Experimental Program. Upon passage of the 1970 Housing Act, the development of an experimental program focusing on key policy questions was begun. First, a detailed conceptual design of an experiment was developed to test systematically the effects of different forms of a housing allowance on household behavior [75]. This evolved into what is now called the Demand Experiment.

In late 1971, the task of developing an initial conceptual design for the measurement of market effects of an allowance program--the Supply Experiment--was begun [74]. As a complementary approach to the estimation of market effects, extensive effort was devoted to the development of a model of urban housing markets that could predict the outcomes of housing allowances and alternative public policies [78]. Third, an approach to gain realistic experience with the administration of an allowance program by various governmental agencies was initiated--an effort now called the Administrative Agency Experiment.

By the spring of 1972, conceptual work was complete and research organizations were selected to operate three separate but interrelated experiments and carry out an integrated analysis of the total program. The combined effort was called the Experimental Housing Allowance Program (EHAP).

Program Design for EHAP

After the decision had been made to conduct three distinct experiments linked together by a common program design, the actual design elements for housing allowances in each of the experiments had to be chosen. Two important considerations were central in planning the experimental allowance programs: (1) the need for an integrated design that would allow consistent policy analysis using data from all three experiments, and (2) legal restrictions on the use of federal funds under which EHAP would be operating. Of particular relevance was the decision that program operating funds for the Administrative Agency and Supply Experiments would come from the Section 23 program.

Table A-1 presents a breakdown of key design elements in each of the three experiments. To facilitate the comparison, the "design center" of the Demand Experiment--in which the design elements are most similar to the program being employed at Supply and Administrative Agency Experiment sites--is used in the table. In the discussion below, however, we will also indicate other program elements tested in the Demand Experiment.

Table A-1

KEY PROGRAM DESIGN ELEMENTS IN THE EXPERIMENTAL HOUSING ALLOWANCE PROGRAM

Design Elements	Demand Experiment	Supply Experiment	Administrative Agency Experiment
Number of Sites	Two	Two	Eight
Administrative Mechanism	Abt Associates, Inc. site office staff	Housing Allowance Office established by The Rand Corporation	Eight public agencies: two each of four types
Scale of Program	1,250 households at each site	(Open enrollment)	400-900 households at each site
Payment Formula	Design center: Housing gap ($P = C^* - bY$) Other variations tested	Housing gap ($P = C^* - bY$)	Housing gap ($P = C^* - bY$)
Definition of Household Unit	Households of two or more related individuals; elderly, disabled or handicapped single persons	Households of two or more related individuals; elderly, disabled or handicapped single persons[a]	Households of two or more related individuals; elderly, disabled or handicapped single persons
Tenure Eligibility	Renters	Homeowners and renters	Renters
Estimate of Rent for Adequate Housing (C^*)	Design center: Panel of experts Percent variations of this estimate tested	Rent survey and Panel of experts	Panel of experts

Table A-1 (continued)

Design Elements	Demand Experiment	Supply Experiment	Administrative Agency Experiment
Household Contribution Rate (b)	Design center: b = .25 Other variations tested	b = .25	b = .25
Income Definition	Gross income minus federal, state and Social Security taxes less $300 annually per wage earner for work-related expenses, other specific deductions	Gross income minus $300 exemption per dependent and each secondary wage earner; 5% standard deduction (10% for elderly); other specific deductions	Gross income minus $300 exemption per dependent and each secondary wage earner; 5% standard deduction (10% for elderly); other specific deductions
Rent Definition	Gross rent or contract rent plus formula-based allowance for utilities paid by household	Gross rent or contract rent plus formula-based allowance for utilities paid by household	Gross rent or contract rent plus formula-based allowance for utilities paid by household
Housing Requirement	Design center: Minimum standards Other variations tested	Minimum standards	Minimum standards
Participant Services	Housing information and equal opportunity support	Housing information and equal opportunity support	Housing information and equal opportunity support

[a]As of August 1, 1977, single-person families with the head of household between 18 and 62 years of age became eligible to receive allowance payments at the two Supply sites; however, the number of households that may receive an allowance is limited to 10 percent of the total recipients authorized under the Annual Contributions Contract.

Both the Demand and Supply Experiments were determined to require the same number of sites--two. The Demand Experiment operated in Pittsburgh, Pennsylvania, and Phoenix, Arizona. The Supply Experiment is operating in Green Bay, Wisconsin, and South Bend, Indiana. The Administrative Agency Experiment, however, included a total of eight sites.[1]

The administrative mechanism used by each experiment also differs. In the Demand Experiment, a research organization--Abt Associates, Incorporated--operated the program; in the Supply Experiment, a non-profit Housing Allowance Office established and controlled by the research contractor, The Rand Corporation, is employed. Since the purpose of the Administrative Agency Experiment is to assess various approaches to the administration of a housing allowance, eight public agencies were chosen to operate the program in these sites. They were: the Housing Authority of the City of Salem, Oregon; the Department of Community Affairs, Commonwealth of Massachusetts; the State of Illinois Department of Local Government Affairs, Office of Housing and Building; the San Bernardino County Board of Supervisors; the Social Services Board of North Dakota; the Jacksonville Department of Housing and Urban Development; the Durham County Department of Social Services; and the Tulsa, Oklahoma Housing Authority.

The scale of the program was set to meet the particular research needs of each experiment. In the Demand Experiment, the number of households

---

[1]These eight sites were Bismarck, North Dakota; Durham, North Carolina; Jacksonville, Florida; Peoria, Illinois; Salem, Oregon; San Bernardino, California; Springfield, Massachusetts, and Tulsa, Oklahoma. In most EHAP sites, the precise program area served includes both the central city and surrounding suburban jurisdictions. At some sites, portions of rural areas are included.

under all of the 17 treatments tested in that experiment were set at about 1,250 in each site. Approximately 500 similar households in each site were enrolled as a control group. They were required to report the same information as the experimental households, including response to baseline and periodic surveys over the course of the experiment. In the Administrative Agency Experiment, the number of recipient households was designed to vary from 400 to 900 at each of the eight sites. The Supply Experiment is, of course, designed to test the market response to a full-scale program. Enrollment at the two Supply sites, therefore, is open to all eligible households.

In designing EHAP, two general methods were identified for establishing a payment formula for determining the amount of a housing allowance to be paid to a particular household: a "housing gap" formula and a "percent of rent" formula.

> The housing gap formula bases the amount of an allowance to be paid to a particular household on the size and income of that household and on local housing market conditions. The formula is calculated so that the household is offered an allowance equal to the difference between market rent for an adequate rental unit of the appropriate size and a percentage of the household's program-defined income.

To clarify, the allowance payment would be calculated as

$$P = C^* - bY,$$

where:
- P = allowance payment,
- C^* = estimate of market rent for adequate housing,
- b = the rate at which the allowance is reduced as income increases (sometimes called a household's contribution rate) and
- Y = program-defined income.

The "percent of rent" formula takes a different approach.

> The percent of rent formula calculates the allowance amount as a fraction of the rent paid by an eligible household. There may be a specified upper limit on rent against which the formula would apply. More complicated versions of this formula might vary the fraction of rent paid according to household size, income and the amount spent on rent.

A simple percent of rent payment can be expressed as

$$P = aR \text{ if } R \leq R^*,$$

where: P = allowance payment,
a = percent of rent paid by government,
R = rent paid by household and
R* = maximum rent upon which an allowance will be paid.

As indicated in Table A-1, the payment formula used in the Supply and Administrative Agency Experiments is the housing gap formula; in the Demand Experiment, the housing gap formula was also used for 12 different treatments, including the center of the design (see Table A-2). In addition, five variations of a simple percent of rent formula were tested in the Demand Experiment, using values of _a_ ranging from .20 to .60.

After considering the formula by which payments are to be calculated, decisions are required on several key definitions and parameter values. First, the household unit definition establishes which households are eligible for the program. In EHAP, essentially the same definition is used in all three experiments. Households are eligible that are composed of two or more related individuals; in addition, households composed of single persons are eligible if the individual is over 61 years of age, disabled or handicapped.[1] This

---

[1]Single-person families with the head of household between 18 and 62 years of age became eligible to receive allowance payments as of August 1, 1977.

Table A-2

THE TWELVE HOUSING GAP ALLOWANCE PLANS TESTED IN THE DEMAND EXPERIMENT
(Housing Gap Formula: $P = C^* - bY$)[a]

Housing Gap Plan	C* Level	b Value	Housing Requirements
1	1.2 C*	.25	Minimum standards
2[b]	C*	.25	Minimum standards
3	0.8 C*	.25	Minimum standards
4	1.2 C*	.25	Minimum rent, low (0.7 C*)
5	C*	.25	Minimum rent, low (0.7 C*)
6	0.8 C*	.25	Minimum rent, low (0.7 C*)
7	1.2 C*	.25	Minimum rent, high (0.9 C*)
8	C*	.25	Minimum rent, high (0.9 C*)
9	0.8 C*	.25	Minimum rent, high (0.9 C*)
10	C*	.15	Minimum standards
11	C*	.35	Minimum standards
12	C*	.25	No requirement

[a]In this formula, P = allowance payment; C* = an estimate of market rent for adequate housing; b = the rate at which the allowance is reduced as income increases (sometimes called a household's contribution rate); and Y = program-defined income.

[b]This plan represents the "design center" of the Demand Experiment, i.e., the plan approximately equivalent to those tested in the other two experiments.

is essentially the definition of household used in the Section 23 program.

Eligibility was also restricted by tenure in the case of the Demand and Administrative Agency Experiments; only renters were eligible in those two experiments. Both renters and homeowners may apply for allowances in the two Supply Experiment sites.

The three parameters in the housing gap formula (C*, b and Y) also require operational meaning in order to establish the precise payment levels to go to participating households. C* estimation techniques varied slightly across the three EHAP experiments. The cost of adequate housing was estimated by bedroom size using the "panel of experts" approach in the Demand and Administrative Agency Experiments. Under this method, "modest neighborhoods" were selected and local realtors, government housing officials, and others with expert knowledge of the local housing market were asked their estimates of market rents by bedroom size for standard housing in each neighborhood. Their responses were used to determine distributions of rent levels. HUD then selected C* values for each bedroom size on the basis of the distributions. Finally, households of different sizes were assumed to require housing units with different numbers of bedrooms.

For the Supply Experiment, a rent survey was conducted as part of an initial screening survey of the local housing market in both sites. It was used as a principal source of information in the determination of C*. In an effort to check the consistency of the rent survey approach with the C* estimated elsewhere, the panel-of-experts technique was used at the first Supply site, Green Bay. The results of the two approaches were broadly consistent.

In the Demand Experiment, 6 of the 12 allowance plans involved testing the use of higher and lower levels of C* than the ones determined by the estimation technique discussed above; three were higher and three were lower.

With respect to establishing b, the "household contribution rate," analyses were carried out on rent-income ratios based on: (1) 1960 and 1970 Census data for households in the income range judged able to consume adequate housing without subsidy (approximately $6,000-$9,000), and (2) a translation of rent-income ratios based on gross census income to a roughly equivalent ratio to the net income definition of the EHAP and (3) an evaluation of the potential cost of national programs at different values of b. Based on this work, b was set at .25 for all household sizes in the Administrative Agency Experiment and the "design center" of the Demand Experiment. Higher and lower values of b, .15 and .35, were also tested in two of the Demand Experiment plans. The Supply Experiment uses b = .25.

The housing gap formula also requires an income definition. This definition varies across experiments, chiefly because of legal restrictions that govern the funding of the Administrative Agency and Supply Experiments. The definition in the Demand Experiment was free of such restrictions and basically involved deducting federal and state income taxes and Social Security taxes from gross income, as well as subtracting $300 per year for work-related expenses of full-time earners within the household. Child-care expenses, extraordinary medical expenses and alimony and support payments were also deducted.

The definition of income used in the Administrative Agency Experiment and Supply Experiment differs from the Demand Experiment primarily in types of deductions. This income definition was essentially imposed on the two experiments because of the reliance on Section 23 program funds. The definition used in these two experiments includes an exemption of $300 for each dependent as well as a $300 exemption for each secondary wage earner. In addition, there are 5-percent standard deductions (10 percent for elderly households) and deductions for child-care, extraordinary medical expenses and alimony.

The rent definition is important for two reasons. First, estimating the cost of adequate housing requires agreement on what constitutes rent. Second, since in all three experiments the allowance payment is not permitted to exceed rent, there must be a standard definition used to calculate rent. Across the three experiments in EHAP, rent is defined in a similar fashion as gross rent, which equals the contract rent plus an additional formula-based allowance for extra costs of utilities paid by the recipient.

A housing allowance is different from unrestricted cash assistance because of housing-related requirements attached to the receipt of the subsidy. Two requirements used in EHAP are minimum standards and minimum rent.

> <u>Minimum standards</u>. When a household is under a minimum standards requirement, it only receives an allowance payment if it rents a housing unit which meets housing standards. Such standards may be based on locally defined codes or on national codes. The requirement could be enforced either through certification by the allowance recipient or his landlord, through inspection by an authorized agency, or through reliance upon the findings of an effective housing code enforcement program.
>
> <u>Minimum rent</u>. A household under a minimum rent requirement must pay for rent a high proportion of the market rent used to calculate its allowance payment. This approach assumes that there is a close correspondence between rent and housing quality.

Both the Supply and Administrative Agency Experiments employ minimum standards requirements. Minimum standards earmarking was also tested at the design center in the Demand Experiment and for varying values for C* and *b*--a total of five plans. In addition, minimum rent requirements were tested in six housing gap treatments in the Demand Experiment. Finally, to provide a benchmark for estimating the effects of requirements, the twelfth housing gap plan provided payments equivalent to those at the design center. A schematic representation of the Demand Experiment design showing the 12 housing gap plans and their variation by C* level, *b* value and housing requirement is presented in Table A-2.

It is not clear that monetary assistance alone will assure that a large number of households obtain housing at a reasonable cost to the government. For many households, income may be the only obstacle to the attainment of decent housing; however, past experience indicates that for many households money is not enough. Two types of participant services are

> *Housing market information*, to assist households in assessing and selecting housing units in terms of structural adequacy, maintenance, financial soundness and landlord-tenant relations.
>
> *Equal opportunity information*, to assist households in combating discrimination in the housing market by race or sex.

Both housing information and equal opportunity information have been provided to participants in EHAP at all 12 sites through housing information sessions. In addition, legal aid and assistance have been available at the sites.

EHAP and the Section 8 (Existing Housing) Program: A Comparison of Features

EHAP and the portion of the ongoing Section 8 program that applies to existing housing share a number of common features: both programs provide cash assistance to low-income households in private rental units; both programs (except for some variations tested in the Demand Experiment of EHAP) require these units to meet program housing standards. Table A-3 provides a comparison of the basic features of the two programs according to program regulations. As the table indicates, the major differences in program features lie in (1) program scale, (2) rent ceiling, (3) homeowner eligibility and (4) direct payment of subsidies to households.

Table A-3

COMPARISON OF EHAP AND THE SECTION 8 (EXISTING HOUSING) PROGRAM:
KEY PROGRAM FEATURES

Program Feature	EHAP	Section 8 Program
Scale of Program	AAE:[a] Agency ceiling on number of recipients Demand: Sample of eligible population made enrollment offer Supply: Open enrollment	Agency ceiling on number of recipients, based on the Annual Contributions Contract
Administering Agencies	AAE: Public agencies (state, local, housing authority and welfare agencies), eight sites Demand and Supply: Research contractors, two sites each	Public housing agencies; HUD may administer where no agency exists
Recipient of Payment	Household	Landlord
Payment Formula	Housing gap[b] $P = C^* - bY$ (percent of rent formula also tested in Demand)	Housing gap with "rent reduction incentive":[c] $P = R - bY + \left(\frac{FMR - R}{FMR}\right) bY$
Household Contribution Rate	b = .25 (.15 and .35 also tested in Demand)	b = .25; (.15 for households in certain categories)[d]
Income Definition	Supply and AAE: Gross income minus $300 exemption for each dependent and secondary wage earner, 5% standard deduction (10% for elderly), and other specific deductions Demand: Gross income minus federal, state and Social Security taxes; less $300 annually per earner for work-related expenses, and other specific deductions	Gross income minus allowances for medical and unusual expenses, less $300 for each minor

Table A-3 (Continued)

Program Feature	EHAP	Section 8 Program
Income Eligibility Limitation (Annual)	Implicit limitation set by payment formula: $Y \leq 4 (C^*) \times 12$ months	80% of median income for program area[e]
Agency Profile Requirement	AAE: Attempt to match the local profile of eligible households Demand and Supply: No profile requirement	At least 30% of households must be "very low-income"
Rent Definition	Gross rent or contract rent plus formula-based allowance for utilities	Gross rent or contract rent plus formula-based allowance for utilities and other services
Rent Limit	None	R typically $\leq$ FMR; some exceptions permitted
Definition of Household Unit	Households of two or more related individuals; elderly, disabled, or handicapped single persons[f]	Households of two or more related individuals; elderly disabled, or handicapped single persons; other persons with special circumstances
Tenure Eligibility	AAE and Demand: Renters Supply: Renters and homeowners	Renters
Locational Restrictions	Households restricted to program sites, which typically encompass multiple political jurisdictions	Households may move to another agency jurisdiction if an interagency cooperation agreement exists
Housing Requirements	Minimum standards: standards may be based on locally defined codes or national model codes (minimum rent also tested in Demand)	Minimum standards: federal performance requirements with acceptability criteria to be fulfilled; may be supplemented by HUD-approved local criteria

Table A-3 (Continued)

Program Feature	EHAP	Section 8 Program
Participant Services	Program information (household), housing information and equal opportunity support	Program information (household and landlord), housing information and equal opportunity support

[a]Administrative Agency Experiment.

[b]P = allowance payment; C* = an estimate of market rent for adequate housing; b = the rate at which the allowance is reduced as income increases (sometimes called a household's contribution rate); and Y = program-defined income. C* varies by number of bedrooms per unit assumed appropriate for families of various sizes.

[c]P = housing subsidy payment; R = gross rent; b = fraction of family income assumed allocated for housing (i.e., household's contribution rate); Y = program-defined income; FMR = fair market rent estimates for adequate housing within program jurisdiction. FMR varies by number of bedrooms per unit assumed appropriate for families of various sizes and by whether or not the structure has an elevator. The "rent reduction incentive" is designed to encourage certified households to search for units that rent below the local FMR, by increasing the monthly subsidy payment by a portion of the difference between contract rent and the FMR.

[d]Three types of families contribute 15% (b = .15) of their gross monthly income: (1) "large, very low-income families," those whose income falls below 50% of median area income with six or more minors in the household; (2) "very large, lower-income families," those whose family includes eight or more minors; (3) "families with exceptionally high medical or other expenses," when such expenses exceed 25% of family gross income.

[e]This figure is for a family of four; the maximum allowable income eligibility is adjusted according to family size.

[f]Effective August 1, 1977, single-person households between 18 and 62 years of age became eligible to receive allowance payments in the two Supply sites; however, the number of these households that may receive payment is limited to 10% of the total recipients authorized for the program under its Annual Contributions Contract.

Appendix B.
REPORT ON EHAP OPERATIONS

Status of EHAP Operations

As of August 1977, about 21,500 households had received at least one housing allowance payment since enrollment in EHAP began in March of 1973. Enrollment is still in progress in only the Supply Experiment; both the Administrative Agency and Demand Experiments have finished the experimental phase in which data were gathered on participating households. About 8,100 families were receiving housing allowances in the Supply Experiment in August 1977.

Administrative Agency Experiment. An enrollment period of up to nine months was used at each of the Administrative Agency Experiment sites; initial enrollment was completed at the last site in May 1974. Only in Jacksonville was the number of participants significantly lower than anticipated. The enrollment period was reopened there to determine whether changes in agency operations could achieve different results. By the end of its second enrollment period, completed in July 1975, the agency was able to obtain the number of participants necessary to reach its target.

The Administrative Agency Experiment was designed to provide two years of allowance payments to families in its experimental phase. The families receiving housing allowances in the experiment received an additional commitment for HUD assistance under the Section 23 leased housing program. This commitment was for three years after the experimental phase ended and is conditional on family eligibility for these programs. All agencies have transferred their responsibilities to local agencies, who are administering programs for the recipient families during the three-year follow-up period.

Table B-1 indicates the status of operations of the Administrative Agency Experiment after the first year of operations in each site, when the experiment was fully operational and before households were phased into other programs. About 6,400 households participated across the eight sites. The average annual adjusted income of participating households was slightly under $3,000, and their average monthly housing allowance payment was about $80.

The Demand Experiment. Enrollment in the Demand Experiment lasted for a ten-month period from April 1973 until February 1974. The experiment provided three years of experimental payments, but these families have an additional two-year commitment from HUD for assistance in transferring to other housing programs where households are eligible. Local site offices set up to administer the experiment in the two sites have completed the transition of households to other housing assistance programs.

The summary status of operations of the Demand Experiment through January 1976--the month prior to the beginning of transition, which occurred after two years of data were collected on participants--is shown in Table B-2. The average payment was $53 in Pittsburgh and $73 in Phoenix.

The Supply Experiment. In the Supply Experiment, open enrollment of households began in June 1974 in Green Bay and in April 1975 in South Bend. Households continue to be enrolled at both sites. During the initial experimental period of up to five years, data are being collected on renters and homeowners. Eligible families may participate throughout the ten-year commitment that HUD has made to each of the communities. This longer period is necessary in the Supply Experiment to determine whether housing suppliers will make capital improvements and other long-term investments.

Table B-1

STATUS OF OPERATIONS OF THE ADMINISTRATIVE AGENCY EXPERIMENT AFTER FIRST YEAR OF OPERATION

Site	Operating Time Period	Recipient Households after First Year of Operation[a]		
		Number	Average Adjusted Income[b] ($)	Average Monthly Payment ($)
Salem, Oregon	March 1973 - December 1975	857	2,800	84
Peoria, Illinois	April 1973 - January 1976	846	3,700	85
Springfield, Massachusetts	April 1973 - February 1976	834	3,000	89
Jacksonville, Florida	April 1973 - July 1977			
	First Enrollment	300	2,000	86
	Second Enrollment	579	3,200	74
San Bernardino, California	May 1973 - March 1976	778	2,900	84
Bismarck, North Dakota	July 1973 - April 1976	389	3,000	72
Durham, North Carolina	July 1973 - May 1976	490	2,400	74
Tulsa, Oklahoma	August 1973 - June 1976	825	2,700	72

[a]This time period represents steady-state operations--when the experiment was fully operational and before households were transferred to other housing programs.

[b]Gross annual income minus deductions for dependents, medical expenses, etc.

Table B-2

STATUS OF OPERATIONS OF THE DEMAND EXPERIMENT
AS OF JANUARY 1976

Site	Operating Time Period	Recipient Households as of January 1976[a]		
		Number[b]	Average Adjusted Income[c] ($)	Average Monthly Payment[d] ($)
Pittsburgh, Pennsylvania	April 1973 - February 1977	667	4,600	53
Phoenix, Arizona	May 1973 - February 1977	546	4,700	73

[a]This time period represents steady-state operations--when the experiment was fully operational and before households began to be transferred to other housing programs.

[b]In addition, there were 119 households in Pittsburgh and 116 households in Phoenix who were on a temporary inactive status as of January 1976. There were also 279 enrolled households in Pittsburgh and 276 enrolled households in Phoenix who did not meet requirements to enable them to receive full payment.

[c]Gross annual income minus federal and state income taxes, social security taxes and allowance for work-related expenses, medical expenses, etc.

[d]These entries are for all households receiving full payments; for recipients of housing gap allowances receiving payments under plans with C* and b most equivalent to the other two experiments, the average monthly payment one year after enrollment was $50 in Pittsburgh, $78 in Phoenix.

The status of operations of the Supply Experiment is shown in Table B-3. As of August 1977, about 8,100 households were receiving housing allowances. About 53 percent of those receiving allowances were homeowners. The average annual income of recipient renters was lower than that of recipient homeowners in both sites; their monthly allowance payments, in turn, were higher.

Table B-3

STATUS OF OPERATIONS OF THE SUPPLY EXPERIMENT
AS OF AUGUST 1977[a]

Site	Operating Time Period[b]	Recipient Households		
		Number	Average Adjusted Income[c] ($)	Average Monthly Payment ($)
Green Bay, Wisconsin	March 1974 - March 1984			
Renters		1,926	3,735	80
Homeowners		1,248	4,174	68
Total		3,174	3,908	75
South Bend, Indiana	September 1974 - September 1984			
Renters		1,881	2,540	88
Homeowners		3,051	3,535	58
Total		4,932	3,155	70

[a]As of August 1, 1977 single-person families with the head of household between 18 and 62 years of age became eligible to receive allowance payments at the two Supply sites; however, the number of households that may receive an allowance is limited to 10 percent of the total recipients authorized under the Annual Contributions Contract.

[b]The time period shown includes an approximate five-year period of experimental data collection and a five-year additional commitment of allowance payments to eligible participating households.

[c]Gross annual income minus deductions for dependents, medical expenses, etc.

MAJOR SOURCES USED IN THE PREPARATION OF THIS PAPER

To synthesize what has been learned throughout the Experimental Housing Allowance Program, the Integrated Analysis relies on various sources of information. They include machine-readable data developed initially as part of the three component experiments or for the Integrated Analysis; analysis reports prepared as part of these experiments and within the Integrated Analysis; and non-experimental data analysis, including simulation modeling. The following are the documents drawn upon most extensively in developing the text and tabular displays in the major sections of this paper. They may be consulted for additional detailed support for many of the findings.

Participation in Housing Allowance Programs

Administrative Agency Experiment [8, 9, 10, 11, 12, 16, 17]

Demand Experiment [23, 24, 25, 27, 31]

Supply Experiment [43]

Integrated Analysis [64, 67]

How Participants Are Assisted by Housing Allowance Programs

Administrative Agency Experiment [9, 15]

Demand Experiment [27, 29, 30]

Supply Experiment [43]

Integrated Analysis [69]

The Effects of Housing Allowances on Markets and Communities

Supply Experiment [43]

Integrated Analysis [63, 65, 66]

Program Administration and Costs

Administrative Agency Experiment [13, 18]

Integrated Analysis [54, 60]

Tables and Figures

Table 1: Administrative Agency Experiment [9, p. 11]; Demand Experiment, derived from special tabulations of December 5, 1975, prepared by Demand Experiment staff; Supply Experiment, derived from [43, p. 80] and Supply Experiment Weekly Status Report of August 12, 1977

Table 2: Administrative Agency Experiment, derived from [12, p. A-8]; Demand Experiment, derived from [23, p. 29]; Supply Experiment, derived from tabulations of Housing Allowance Office records through June 1976 in Green Bay and December 1976 in South Bend, specified by Integrated Analysis staff and prepared by Supply Experiment staff

Table 3: Administrative Agency Experiment, tabulations by Integrated Analysis staff from Agency Operating Form data files; Demand Experiment, derived from [31, p. 23]; Supply Experiment, tabulations by Integrated Analysis staff from Supply Experiment Weekly Status Report of August 12, 1977

Table 4: Administrative Agency Experiment, tabulations by Integrated Analysis staff from Agency Operating Form data files; Demand Experiment, derived from [23, p. 29]; Supply Experiment, derived from tabulation of Housing Allowance Office records through June 1976 in Green Bay and December 1976 in South Bend, specified by Integrated Analysis staff and prepared by Supply Experiment staff

Table 5: Demand Experiment, derived from [27, pp. 91, 95]

Table 6: Administrative Agency Experiment, tabulations by Integrated Analysis staff from Agency Operating Form data files; Demand Experiment, derived from [27, pp. A-47, A-48, A-50 and A-51]; Supply Experiment, derived from tabulations of Housing Allowance Office records through June 1976 in Green Bay and December 1976 in South Bend, specified by Integrated Analysis staff and prepared by Supply Experiment staff

Table 7: Supply Experiment, derived from special tabulations of January 4, 1978, prepared by Supply Experiment staff

Table 8: Administrative Agency Experiment, tabulations by Integrated Analysis staff from [13, pp. 26-28, 79, 139]

Table 9: Tabulations by Integrated Analysis staff by adjusting simulation reported in [60, p. 27]; estimates adjusted to reflect use of "net" rather than "gross" income, to exclude non-elderly, single-person households and to reflect EHAP participation experience in Green Bay as of early 1977

Tables and Figures (continued)

Figure 2: Administrative Agency Experiment, tabulations by Integrated Analysis staff from Agency Operating Form data files, Demand Experiment, derived from [27, p. 22]; Supply Experiment, derived from table, "Major Paths to First Certification," presented as part of a Supply Experiment seminar, "Two Years of Housing Allowances," held in Washington, D.C., on September 28, 1977

SELECTED BIBLIOGRAPHY

Of necessity, this paper does not incorporate all aspects of the EHAP research agenda. Readers who are interested in additional detail on the findings cited in this paper or in other areas of EHAP research should consult the selected list of reports below. Some documents can be obtained by contacting the National Technical Information Service, Springfield, Virginia, 22161. NTIS document numbers are noted.

Asterisks appear before items added after the bibliography of Housing Allowances: The 1976 Report to Congress, U.S. Department of Housing and Urban Development, Office of Policy Development and Research, Washington, D.C., February 1976. Findings have been included in the annotations of many of these recent items.

General

1. First Annual Report of the Experimental Housing Allowance Program, U.S. Department of Housing and Urban Development, Office of Policy Development and Research, Washington, D.C., May 1973 (PB 241490).

    A description of the overall goals and design of EHAP and the program's status as of early 1973. This report was prepared for and submitted to Congress pursuant to Section 504 of the Housing and Urban Development Act of 1970, which directed HUD to establish the Experimental Housing Allowance Program. An appendix describes housing allowance experiences in seven European countries.

2. Second Annual Report on the Experimental Housing Allowance Program, U.S. Department of Housing and Urban Development, Office of Policy Development and Research, Washington, D.C., June 1974 (PB 244218).

    A description of EHAP activities between May 1973 and June 1974, including initial operational activities. This report was prepared for and submitted to Congress pursuant to Section 504 of the Housing and Urban Development Act of 1970. Preliminary impressions from the Kansas City, Missouri and Wilmington, Delaware demonstration housing allowance programs are included.

3. Experimental Housing Allowance Program: Initial Impressions and Findings, Interim Report, U.S. Department of Housing and Urban Development, Office of Policy Development and Research, Washington, D.C., April 1975 (PB 245815).

A discussion of early EHAP findings on two topics. The first focuses on basic information on the more than 10,000 households that had received allowance payments from EHAP by April 1975. Areas covered include household characteristics, amount and sources of income and housing conditions prior to receiving program payments. The second topic discussed is preliminary findings from the Administrative Agency Experiment on the enrollment process.

4. Housing Allowances: The 1976 Report to Congress, U.S. Department of Housing and Urban Development, Office of Policy Development and Research, Washington, D.C., February 1976 (PB 263656).

A report on what has been learned from 2.5 years of testing the housing allowance concept, prepared for and submitted to Congress pursuant to Section 804 of the Housing and Urban Development Act of 1974. The report investigates evidence from the early years of the program on the feasibility of the housing allowance approach as a way of assisting low-income households and the status of continuing EHAP research, including some preliminary findings.

Administrative Agency Experiment

5. Agency Program Manual, Abt Associates, Inc., Cambridge, Massachusetts, Revised, March 1973 (PB 241992).

A description of the scheduling and planning requirements that HUD imposed upon the eight administering agencies of the Administrative Agency Experiment in developing their policies and procedures to operate the experiment. The document includes the program functions that agencies were required to implement.

6. Summary Evaluation Plan of the Administrative Agency Experiment, Abt Associates, Inc., Cambridge, Massachusetts, January 1973 (PB 241555).

A summary of methodology initially planned for evaluating the Administrative Agency Experiment. The document explains the functions to be evaluated and describes the analysis plans and how they address policy issues specified by HUD.

7. First Annual Report of the Administrative Agency Experiment, Abt Associates, Inc., Cambridge, Massachusetts, May 1974 (PB 241545).

An overview of activities from September 1972 to September 1973 in the Administrative Agency Experiment. The report includes a description of the various agencies' approaches to meeting HUD's operational requirements.

8. Second Annual Report of the Administrative Agency Experiment, Abt Associates, Inc., Cambridge, Massachusetts, December 1974 (PB 241544).

A description of the operations, the participating agencies and the status of the evaluation activities through the end of the second year of the experiment, October 1974.

*9. Third Annual Report of the Administrative Agency Experiment Evaluation, Frederick T. Temple, William L. Holshouser, Jr., M. G. Trend, David W. Budding and Mireille L. Ernst, Abt Associates, Inc., Cambridge, Massachusetts, August 1976 (PB 265648).

A report on the final operational phase of the Administrative Agency Experiment. The document provides summary statistics describing the experiences of participating families. It considers the three major stages of a household's program experience: entering the program, becoming a recipient, and the first year of full participation.

*10. Report on Selected Aspects of the Jacksonville Housing Allowance Experiment, William L. Holshouser, Jr., Abt Associates, Inc., Cambridge, Massachusetts, May 1976 (PB 265654).

This report is based upon an analysis undertaken when it became clear that the experiences of the Jacksonville agency differed significantly from those of the other administrative agencies. The report addresses two aspects of the Jacksonville experience: (1) the limited and unrepresentative response of the eligible population in applying to the program, and (2) the failure of significant numbers of black families to participate successfully in the program.

*11. Jacksonville: Administering a Housing Allowance Program in a Difficult Environment, Marian F. Wolfe and William L. Hamilton et al., Abt Associates, Inc., Cambridge, Massachusetts, February 1977 (PB 265673).

The results of administrative changes introduced during a second enrollment period in Jacksonville. The Jacksonville agency succeeded in obtaining the target number of recipients, and the proportion of enrollees who became recipients rose from 33 percent to 50 percent. Black enrollees, however, were less successful than whites. Much of the problem can be attributed to housing market conditions, combined with a rigorously enforced housing standard and a low level of supportive services to enrollees. Although the agency attempted to reduce supplier resistance to the program during the second enrollment period, the general stability of family dropout rates during both periods indicates that these efforts had little effect on program results.

*12. Outreach: Generating Applications in the Administrative Agency Experiment, Jean MacMillan and William L. Hamilton et al., Abt Associates, Inc., Cambridge, Massachusetts, February 1977 (PB 265683).

An analysis of the Administrative Agency Experiment's experience in outreach. The advantages and disadvantages of the various agency outreach procedures are examined. Two questions are addressed: how did eligible households respond to the program, and what effect did the agencies' outreach techniques have on that response? Despite agency efforts to attract a representative cross-section of all those eligible, some households were more likely to apply than others. The elderly and working poor were underrepresented, while the welfare population was overrepresented compared to the eligible population.

Elderly households were less likely to hear about the program and apply than other groups. Forty-two percent of the welfare households who knew of the program applied, compared to 28 percent of the working poor, which tends to support the idea that a stigma is attached to assistance programs.

*13. Administrative Costs in a Housing Allowance Program: Two-Year Costs in the Administrative Agency Experiment, Charles M. Maloy, J. Patrick Madden, David W. Budding and William L. Hamilton, Abt Associates, Inc., Cambridge, Massachusetts, February 1977 (PB 265675).

A review of the administrative costs of the eight agencies of the Administrative Agency Experiment during the first two years of program operations. Since HUD permitted variation in program design and operation within broad federal guidelines, administrative costs varied across agencies. The report discusses these actual cost variations and pinpoints where policy decisions are likely to affect administrative costs. The report distinguishes direct costs, such as intake (incurred to bring households into the program) and maintenance (to provide ongoing services to recipients) from indirect costs, such as overhead, maintenance, record-keeping and office space. Several areas where policy decisions might be particularly influential are identified: outreach, enrollee and recipient services and housing inspections.

*14. Certification: Determining Eligibility and Setting Payment Levels in the Administrative Agency Experiment, Donald E. Dickson, Jr. et al., Abt Associates, Inc., Cambridge, Massachusetts, March 1977 (PB 265695).

An examination of household eligibility criteria and procedures used in the Administrative Agency Experiment. Across agencies, a median of 8 percent of all applicants were found ineligible after screening and certification and slightly less than half of these applicants were ineligible because their income exceeded program limits. Certification resulted in changes in household size data in only about 5 percent of all cases, although in general the agencies were not stringent in certifying household size data. Income data frequently changed as a result of certification; overall, changes were recorded in 51 percent of the cases. Documentation or verification by third-party sources resulted in more changes in income data than self-declaration by participants. The longer the interval between application and certification, the more often a change was recorded, both in income and household size.

*15. Supportive Services in the Administrative Agency Experiment, William L. Holshouser, Jr. et al., Abt Associates, Inc., Cambridge, Massachusetts, February 1977 (PB 265655).

An analysis of agency supportive services intended to help participants meet the requirements of the program and make better use of their subsidy. The report investigates the effect of both "formal" services (information sessions) and "responsive" services (made available as problems arise), such as transportation to search for a new unit, assistance in negotiating lease provisions or repairs with landlords, etc. Services were found to be most effective in helping enrollees qualify as recipients in tighter housing markets, particularly for households that attempted to move and for black households, whether or not they attempted to move. Although services were important for enrollees, there is little evidence that those services made a difference once they became recipients.

*16. Inspection: Implementing Housing Quality Requirements in the Administrative Agency Experiment, David W. Budding et al., Abt Associates, Inc., Cambridge, Massachusetts, February 1977 (PB 266095).

A detailed analysis of agency inspection procedures used to administer the housing standards requirement. The standards developed by the agencies differed considerably in the number and nature of items included, in the measurement of particular housing attributes, and in the types of inspectors employed to administer the standards. Professional inspectors were the most effective. Staff members were found to be effective if they received extensive training and had no other responsibilities. The more training they received, the greater their similarity to the professionals. Participant inspection proved least effective, although the estimated cost was about one-third of that for the other types of inspection.

*17. Elderly Participants in the Administrative Agency Experiment, Marian F. Wolfe, William L. Hamilton and M. G. Trend and Bradford S. Wild, Abt Associates, Inc., Cambridge, Massachusetts, March 1977 (PB 265685).

An examination of the experiences of elderly households in the Administrative Agency Experiment, contrasted with the experiences of non-elderly households. Overall, there were more similarities than differences. The housing allowance helped both groups achieve some reduction of their rent burden, improvement in the physical quality of their housing, reduction in crowded housing conditions and improvements in their neighborhoods. There were also some significant differences between the results for elderly and non-elderly. The elderly had lower participation rates, greater average reductions in their rent burden and a relatively high success rate in meeting housing quality requirements and becoming recipients. Special administrative procedures were required for the elderly in the areas of outreach, income certification and supportive services.

*18. Administrative Procedures in a Housing Allowance Program: The Administrative Agency Experiment, William L. Hamilton, David W. Budding and William L. Holshouser, Jr., Abt Associates, Inc., Cambridge, Massachusetts, March 1977 (PB 265635).

An examination of alternative procedures for local administration of a housing allowance program, based largely on earlier reports on individual administrative functions. Program effectiveness was significantly affected in the Administrative Agency Experiment by the choice among procedures for developing four administrative functions: outreach, certification of applicants' reported income, inspection of participants' dwelling units and supportive services. For all functions except certification, the choice of procedures also significantly influenced administrative costs. Although the agencies performed the functions of screening and selection, enrollment and payment operations differently, the various procedures used made little difference in either cost or effectiveness. This analysis of alternative procedures focuses on four experiment concerns: patterns of program participation, agency enforcement of program requirements, the extent of improvement in participants' housing conditions and administrative costs.

Demand Experiment

19. Experimental Design and Analysis Plan of the Demand Experiment, Abt Associates, Inc., Cambridge, Massachusetts, Revised, August 1973 (PB 239507).

A discussion of the design and evaluation plan for the Demand Experiment, with explanation of program treatment plans that families must follow to receive cash subsidies and how these treatment and analysis plans address policy issues identified by HUD.

20. Evaluation Design: Executive Summary, Abt Associates, Inc., Cambridge, Massachusetts, June 1973 (PB 241031).

A condensed description of the essential components of the experimental design and analysis plan of the Demand Experiment.

21. First Annual Report of the Demand Experiment, Abt Associates, Inc., Cambridge, Massachusetts, March 1974 (PB 239598).

A summary of first-year Demand Experiment activities, including an overall description of the organization of the experiment and major developments in design, analysis and data processing.

22. Second Annual Report of the Demand Experiment, Abt Associates, Inc., Cambridge, Massachusetts, February 1975 (PB 241032).

A summary of the activities of the Demand Experiment during 1974 and an outline of plans for 1975, including a description of the families enrolled in the experiment and a comparison of enrolled families with census-based estimates of the eligible families in Pittsburgh and Phoenix, the two Demand sites.

*23. Third Annual Report of the Demand Experiment, Abt Associates, Inc., Cambridge, Massachusetts, October 1976 (PB 265971).

A summary of the activities of the Demand Experiment from January 1, 1975 through December 31, 1975. During this period, major emphasis was placed on four areas: analysis, program operations, data base development and experimental design. On the basis of preliminary tabulation of the data, allowances apparently have not substantially altered patterns of locational choices among participants, and there has been little change in racial or socioeconomic concentrations. As expected, allowances have affected participants differently, depending on their initial housing status. Operational activity of 1975 involved planning for the termination of participants that was to begin in 1976.

*24. Fourth Annual Report of the Demand Experiment, Abt Associates, Inc., Cambridge, Massachusetts (Forthcoming).

A summary of the activities of the Demand Experiment for 1976 and plans for early 1977. The period covered represents a milestone in the completion of the Demand Experiment. Data collection was completed in mid-1976 and program operations phased out during 1976 and 1977. By early 1977, preliminary analysis of the first year of program operations was complete. A summary of that analysis is included, with overall patterns of results covering participant response to housing allowances, increases in housing expenditures, locational choice and proportion of households meeting the various housing requirements.

25. Working Paper on Early Findings: Demand Experiment, Experimental Housing Allowance Program, Abt Associates, Inc., Cambridge, Massachusetts, January 1975 (PB 242002).

A description of the initial (baseline) position of households enrolled in the Demand Experiment sites drawn from participant interviews and housing evaluations. The document includes demographic descriptions of the enrolled population, a preliminary examination of factors involved in the enrollment decision, and an examination of cross-sectional data on enrollees and their housing (housing conditions, expenditures, locations, and enrollees' satisfaction with their housing at the outset of the experiment).

*26. Housing Expenditures and Quality, Part I: Report on Housing Expenditures under a Percent of Rent Housing Allowance, Stephen K. Mayo, Abt Associates, Inc., Cambridge, Massachusetts, January 1977 (PB 265933).

A discussion of one type of housing allowance payment formula being tested in the Demand Experiment, a subsidy under which households receive an amount equal to a percentage of their monthly rental expenditures. The subsidy is aimed at encouraging households to increase expenditures on housing, which in turn should increase housing quality. This report analyzes changes in housing consumption patterns of participants during the first year of the Demand Experiment, particularly changes in rental expenditures.

*27. Housing Expenditures and Quality, Part II: Report on Housing Expenditures under a Housing Gap Housing Allowance, Joseph Friedman and Stephen D. Kennedy, Abt Associates, Inc., Cambridge, Massachusetts, May 1977.

An analysis of changes in the housing expenditures of recipients of housing gap housing allowances in the Demand Experiment, compared to their predicted usual spending in the absence of the allowances. Two major findings derived from first-year data are (1) recipients that met the housing requirements only after enrollment increased their housing expenditures by much more than recipients that already met the requirements at enrollment; the latter group appeared to respond to allowances about the same as they would to any other income increase, and (2) more than one-half of allowance recipients met requirements at enrollment; of the remainder--the group that met requirements only after enrollment--about half were estimated to have been directly induced by the program to meet them. This proportion may increase over time, however, as more households move.

*28. Housing Expenditures and Quality Part III: Report on Hedonic Indices as a Measure of Housing Quality, Sally R. Merrill, Abt Associates, Inc., Cambridge, Massachusetts (Forthcoming).

A discussion focusing on the hedonic index approach to measurement of housing quality. This paper describes a housing index derived from the Demand Experiment's hedonic model of housing and uses the model to analyze and test the index with experimental data from Pittsburgh and Phoenix, over time and across submarkets. Several topics are explored to develop a greater understanding of the model and these data, such as price discrimination against minorities, housing market segmentation and the discount associated with long-term residence in a rental unit. The results of the paper show that meaningful measures of housing quality can be derived through use of this hedonic index approach.

*29. Locational Choice Part I: Search and Mobility in the Housing Allowance Demand Experiment, Daniel Weinberg, Reilly Atkinson, Avis Vidal, James E. Wallace and Glen Weisbrod, Abt Associates, Inc., Cambridge, Massachusetts, August 1977 (PB 273308).

An analysis of the first-year search and moving behavior of participants in the Demand Experiment, using multivariate statistical techniques and examination of interview responses. The allowance programs offered in the Demand Experiment apparently had little or no overall effect on moving. Examination of the search decision includes the reasons cited for not searching and the effects of dissatisfaction and housing conditions on search. Moving behavior of searchers is discussed with emphasis on the search process and the problems encountered by households. The investigation also includes the relationship between the incidence of these problems and both household characteristics and effect of search problems on moving rates.

*30. Locational Choice Part II: Neighborhood Change in the Housing Allowance Demand Experiment, Reilly Atkinson and Antony Phipps, Abt Associates, Inc. Cambridge, Massachusetts, August 1977.

An analysis of the first-year neighborhood changes of participants in the Demand Experiment, using census data on low-income households and minority households in the origin and destination census tracts of movers. The analysis of program effects is limited and, in some cases, sharply curtailed by small sample sizes. The results suggest that a housing allowance does not have a major influence on the locational choices of participants or the residential distribution of the low-income or minority population. The findings are generally consistent with the experience of housing allowance demonstrations in Kansas City, Missouri, Wilmington, Delaware and the eight cities involved in the Administrative Agency Experiment.

*31. Report on Participation under a Housing Gap Form of Housing Allowance, Stephen D. Kennedy, T. Krishna Kumar and Glen Weisbrod, Abt Associates, Inc. Cambridge, Massachusetts (Forthcoming).

Development of a theoretical model of factors affecting household participation behavior in the Demand Experiment. Participation is considered in two phases: acceptance of an enrollment offer and subsequent participation, subject to fulfillment of housing requirements. First-year data are found to confirm the general structure of the model. The analysis yields estimates of the effect on participation rates of alternative payment levels and alternative housing requirements as well as the demographic characteristics of eligible households.

Supply Experiment

32. General Design Report: First Draft, Ira S. Lowry (ed.), The Rand Corporation, Santa Monica, California, May 1973 (PB 242033).

33. General Design Report: Supplement, Ira S. Lowry (ed.), The Rand Corporation, Santa Monica, California, August 1973 (PB 242031).

34. Proceedings of the General Design Review of the Housing Assistance Supply Experiment, The Rand Corporation, Santa Monica, California, October 1973 (PB 242273).

35. Monitoring the Experiment: An Update of Section IV of the General Design Report, Ira S. Lowry, The Rand Corporation, Santa Monica, California, April 1975.

36. The Experimental Housing Allowance Program: An Update of Section III of the General Design Report, Ira S. Lowry, The Rand Corporation, Santa Monica, California, April 1975.

37. Introduction and Overview: An Update of Sections I and II of the General Design Report, Ira S. Lowry, The Rand Corporation, Santa Monica, California, May 1975.

38. Market Intermediaries and Indirect Suppliers: Baseline Report and Prospects for Site I, William G. Grigsby, Michael G. Shanley and Sammis B. White, The Rand Corporation, Santa Monica, California, February 1974 (PB 246749).

39. Market Intermediaries and Indirect Suppliers: Reconnaissance and Research Design for Site II, William G. Grigsby, Michael G. Shanley and Sammis B. White, The Rand Corporation, Santa Monica, California, May 1975.

*40. Using Hedonic Indexes To Measure Supply Response to Housing Allowances, C. Lance Barnett, The Rand Corporation, Santa Monica, California, August 1976.

These documents (numbers 32-40), taken together, describe the design of the Supply Experiment and analysis plans to be used in the preparation of reports on findings of the experiment.

*41. First Annual Report of the Housing Assistance Supply Experiment, The Rand Corporation, Santa Monica, California, October 1974 (PB 241701).

A summary of the history and design of the Supply Experiment. The report describes the implementation and achievements of the experiment through September 1974; it discusses current problems and explains the schedule of future events.

*42. Second Annual Report of the Housing Assistance Supply Experiment, The Rand Corporation, Santa Monica, California, May 1976 (PB 266244).

A summary of the baseline (or preintervention) status of the Green Bay and South Bend metropolitan housing market, with preliminary findings from the first year of program operation in Green Bay. As a continuation of the historical account of the Supply Experiment, the report also summarizes progress in the two experimental sites during the period October 1, 1974 through September 30, 1975.

*43. Third Annual Report of the Housing Assistance Supply Experiment, The Rand Corporation, Santa Monica, California, February 1977 (PB 266245).

A description of the progress of the Supply Experiment during its third year of field operations, October 1975 through September 1976. The report compares research findings for the two Supply Experiment sites, relates the characteristics of each local housing market before the allowance program began, discusses the characteristics and experiences of those who have enrolled in the programs and summarizes the effects of each program on its participants and on the market and community in which it operates.

44. Rental Housing in Site I: Characteristics of the Capital Stock at Baseline, C. Peter Rydell, The Rand Corporation, Santa Monica, California August 1975 (PB 245853).

An analysis of the characteristics of the capital stock of rental housing in Brown County, Wisconsin, in 1973. This document is an exploratory study to determine whether the various combinations of land and physical improvements in rental properties in Brown County conform to general principles from the economic theory of production.

45. Rental Housing in Site I: Market Structure and Conditions at Baseline, C. Peter Rydell and Joseph Friedman, The Rand Corporation, Santa Monica, California, April 1975 (PB 246747).

An investigation of characteristics of the 1973 rental housing market in Brown County, Wisconsin. Market "tightness" is measured and submarkets identified for special attention when supply response to the program is later analyzed.

*46. Housing Choices and Residential Mobility in Site I at Baseline, Kevin F. McCarthy, The Rand Corporation, Santa Monica, California, August 1976 (PB 266168).

An examination of the relationship between household characteristics and housing choices among households in Green Bay before the onset of the housing allowance program. The description of general characteristics of households is based on a life-cycle classification that groups households according to marital status, ages of household heads, presence of children, and age of youngest child. Household characteristics, including size, labor force participation and income, are shown to vary with life-cycle stage in patterns indicating that household needs, as well as the households' financial ability to meet these needs, vary systematically over the life cycle. These patterns can be perceived in housing choices: tenure, type and size of unit, housing expenditures and residential mobility.

*47. Market Intermediaries and Indirect Suppliers: First Year Report for Site I, Sammis B. White, The Rand Corporation, Santa Monica, California, September 1976 (PB 266141).

An assessment of the effects of the first year of housing allowances at the Green Bay site on the activities and attitudes of mortgage lenders, real estate brokers and home repair contractors. Since there were few transactions between program participants and the first two groups, little effect was discerned. During the program's first year more than 800 housing units were repaired or improved to qualify them for occupancy by allowance recipients but the effects of this activity on the home repair industry, according to the report, were also insignificant.

Integrated Analysis

48. Integrated Analysis of the Experimental Housing Allowance Program, The Urban Institute, Washington, D.C., November 1973 (PB 249914).

49. Integrated Analysis of the Experimental Housing Allowance Program: Supplement, The Urban Institute, Washington, D.C., December 1973 (PB 249868).

50. The Process of Housing Choice: Conceptual Background and Research Plans, John L. Goodman, Jr., and Mary Vogel, assisted by Mark P. Berkman, The Urban Institute, Washington, D.C., February 1975 (PB 249875).

51. Data Sources for the Integrated Analysis, C. Reid Melton, assisted by James L. Cogley and Susan Anderson, The Urban Institute, Washington, D.C., February 1975 (PB 249871).

52. A Framework for the Analysis of Income Accounting Systems in EHAP, James P. Zais, C. Reid Melton and Mark P. Berkman, The Urban Institute, Washington, D.C., July 1975 (PB 249871).

53. Integrating the Supply Experiment and the Housing Market Model, Larry J. Ozanne, The Urban Institute, Washington, D.C., July 1975 (PB 249873).

*54. Integrated Analysis of Administration of Housing Allowance Programs, James P. Zais and John W. Trutko, The Urban Institute, Washington, D.C., September 1976.

These papers (numbers 48-54), taken together, describe the design of the Integrated Analysis of EHAP. This approach emphasizes seven components--national costs and benefits, housing quality, prices and market effects, housing choice process, income accounting, program integration, and program administration. The component analyses in the design are important in assessing the implications of a national housing program.

55. Integrated Design and Evaluation of the Experimental Housing Allowance Program: First Year Report, The Urban Institute, Washington, D.C., May 1973 (PB 249867).

56. The Experimental Housing Allowance Program: Second Year Report, The Urban Institute, Washington, D.C., September 1974 (PB 249915).

57. Integrated Analysis of the Experimental Housing Allowance Program: Third Year Report, The Urban Institute, Washington, D.C., June 1975 (PB 247775).

*58. Integrated Analysis of the Experimental Housing Allowance Program: Fourth Year Report, The Urban Institute, Washington, D.C., January 1977 (PB 249914).

These papers (numbers 55-58) describe work carried out by The Urban Institute from 1972 through 1976 on the development of an integrated program and research design for the analysis of issues across the experimental elements of EHAP. The last paper in this series includes a summary of overall findings of EHAP research.

59. Simulations of National Housing Allowances: An Application of the TRIM Model, Ronald J. Sepanik, Gary Hendricks and John D. Heinberg, The Urban Institute, Washington, D.C., February 1975 (PB 249874).

60. Variations of Selective Design Elements for Housing Allowances: Simulations Using the TRIM Model, Ronald J. Sepanik, The Urban Institute, Washington, D.C., August 1975 (PB 249869).

These two papers (numbers 59-60) document how The Urban Institute TRIM Model was adapted to enable estimates of costs and benefit patterns of a national housing allowance program and discuss the consequences of changing certain key program elements of a national housing allowance design.

61. The Missing Piece to the Puzzle? Housing Allowances and the Welfare System, John D. Heinberg, Joanne D. Culbertson and James P. Zais, assisted by Barry L. Friedman, Leonard J. Hausman and Joseph J. Valenza, The Urban Institute, Washington, D.C., December 1974 (PB 249866).

62. Integrating a Housing Allowance with the Welfare System: Further Analysis of Program-Linking Strategies and Joint Administration, John D. Heinberg, Joanne D. Culbertson, Margaret J. Drury and James P. Zais, The Urban Institute, Washington, D.C., November 1975 (PB 249872).

These two papers (numbers 61-62) address major aspects of integrating housing allowances with other income-conditioned transfer programs. Emphasis is on the problem of linking the benefit structure of a housing allowance with that of other programs and the administrative arrangements for coordinating or sharing of administrative functions across programs.

*63. Experimental Testing of Housing Allowances: Evidence of Program Feasibility and Other Preliminary Findings, James P. Zais, John D. Heinberg and Margaret J. Drury, The Urban Institute, Washington, D.C., February 1976.

A synthesis and appraisal of findings from 2.5 years of testing the housing allowance concept through operation of EHAP. The format of the report was developed to facilitate a report by HUD to the Congress. (See number 4 above).

*64. Housing Allowances and Local Area Variation in Residential Mobility, John L. Goodman, Jr., The Urban Institute, Washington, D.C., June 1976.

An analysis of the role played by residential mobility in a housing allowance program and how that role can be expected to vary across local program areas. The analysis includes the relationship between selected housing market variables and local mobility rates. The major findings of the paper are: (1) residential mobility greatly increases the chances of attaining housing that meets the housing quality requirements for those renter households who did not meet requirements at enrollment; (2) substantial variation across EHAP sites can be expected in the mobility of enrolled households during the experiments; (3) population mobility rates are insensitive to local, market-wide housing vacancy rates or to the level of urbanization; and (4) mobility rates are highest in growing counties and urbanized areas. The paper explores several implications of these findings for a housing allowance program. First, the importance of moving vis-a-vis upgrading the current dwelling unit to meet the housing quality requirement will vary by program site. Second, since homeowners do not frequently move to improve housing, of the approximately 40 percent of the national program-eligible population who own homes, relatively few would meet the housing requirement by moving.

*65. The Urban Institute Housing Model: Application to South Bend, Indiana, Sue A. Marshall, The Urban Institute, Washington, D.C., June 1976.

*66. The Urban Institute Housing Model: Application to Green Bay, Wisconsin, Jean E. Vanski, The Urban Institute, Washington, D.C., June 1976.

These two papers (numbers 65-66) describe applications of The Urban Institute's Housing Market Model to South Bend, Indiana, and Green Bay, Wisconsin. The model simulates interactions in the housing market among model households dwellings (controlled by housing suppliers), new construction, and governmental policies. As a first stage in integrating the model with the Supply Experiment, the model was calibrated to each experimental site using data for the 1960-1970 decade.

*67. Program Housing Standards in the Experimental Housing Allowance Program: Analyzing Differences in the Demand and Supply Experiments, Joseph E. Valenza, The Urban Institute, Washington, D.C., July 1977.

An analysis of housing quality standards as currently applied in the Demand and Supply Experiments. The results indicate that, first, more housing units were unacceptable according to Demand Experiment standards in a jointly evaluated sample of units than units judged by Supply Experiment standards. Second, different aspects of the program standards caused the majority of failures under the different standards as implemented. And third, the physical conditions of the units evaluated did not vary significantly between the sites of the two experiments. Differences in program standards, rather than differences in pre-experimental housing stock, caused the failure rate for units evaluated by the Demand Experiment standards to be higher than when the Supply Experiment standards are used. The paper also explores how differences in program standards are likely to lead to different behavioral responses from eligible households.

*68. Generalizing from the Experimental Housing Allowance Program: An Assessment of Site Representativeness, Jeanne E. Goedert, The Urban Institute, Washington, D.C., July 1976.

An investigation of EHAP site characteristics, using 1970 Census tabulations, to determine how those sites compare to the nation's other urbanized areas. Preliminary research indicates that, other things being equal, household success in meeting allowance program housing standards is a positive function of their initial housing conditions (assumed in this study to be correlated with the quality of housing stock, as measured by presence of complete plumbing and percentage of housing units built after 1940--and with the absence of of overcrowding) and the potential mobility rate of eligible households (assumed to be positively correlated with past rates of intracounty mobility; negatively correlated with the percentages of the population that are black, Spanish, elderly and percentage female-headed households; and positively correlated with the availability of housing units, as measured by the vacancy rates of rental units). The 12 EHAP sites tested are found to represent a reasonable range and distribution of these housing and household characteristics in terms of other urbanized areas. The range of values observed across the sites should typify all but the extreme values one would observe for other urbanized areas on variables hypothesized to influence the ability of households to qualify for housing allowance payments.

The study also examines the degree of contrast offered by the two Supply Experiment sites on variables considered to influence the magnitude of increases in the price per unit of housing services brought about by a housing allowance program. It appears that such increases may be low in Green Bay and about average in South Bend compared to other urbanized areas.

*69. Housing Allowances and Residential Mobility: An Interim Report, John L. Goodman, Jr., The Urban Institute, Washington, D.C., October 1976.

Preliminary findings on eligible EHAP households that move to attain housing that meets minimum quality standards, on whether or not their decisions to move are induced by the program, and on the locations selected by those who move. Early data from the Demand and Administrative Agency Experiments indicate that moving plays a prominent role in the attainment of housing that meets program standards, although there is considerable variation across sites in the relative importance of mobility. A housing allowance program may influence the decision to look for another place, the method of search, the ultimate decision of searchers to move or stay and the characteristics of the housing selected by movers. For many households, moving is necessary for improvement of their housing situations. However, moving does not guarantee housing improvement. The study outlines current and future research needed to develop a more thorough understanding of mobility and its role in a housing allowance program.

*70. Indicators of the Quality of U.S. Housing, Jeanne E. Goedert and John L. Goodman, Jr., The Urban Institute, Washington, D.C., September 1977.

Development of a set of indicators of housing quality using the 1973 Annual Housing Survey and a description of occupied housing in the United States in terms of those indicators. The analysis shows that the deficiencies noted in occupied U.S. housing are distributed widely across units and are not clustered in a small number of seriously dilapidated units. There are higher incidences of housing deficiencies in rural housing, as compared with urban housing, and in rental units relative to owner-occupied units. The results also imply that it will be difficult to find any simple measure that captures the many dimensions of housing quality. It is shown that no item from an extensive list of housing characteristics clearly distinguished the housing of low-income households from that of higher-income families, nor does one characteristic serve as a proxy for a variety of other housing features.

Background Studies

71. The Design of a Housing Allowance, Frank de Leeuw, Sam H. Leaman and Helen Blank, The Urban Institute, Washington, D.C., October 1970.

72. The Transfer Cost of a Housing Allowance: Conceptual Issues and Benefit Patterns, John D. Heinberg, The Urban Institute, Washington, D.C., May 1971.

73. "The Housing Allowance Approach" (reprint from _Papers Submitted to Subcommittee on Housing Panels_, Part 2, Committee on Banking and Currency, House of Representatives, Washington, D.C., June 1971) Frank de Leeuw, The Urban Institute, Washington, D.C., June 1971.

74. _Testing the Supply Response to Housing Allowances: An Experimental Design_, Ira S. Lowry, C. Peter Rydell and David M. de Ferranti, The Rand Corporation, Santa Monica, California, December 1971.

75. _Housing Allowance Household Experiment Design: Part I - Summary and Overview_, Garth Buchanan and John D. Heinberg, The Urban Institute, Washington, D.C., May 1972.

76. "Time Lags in the Rental Housing Market" (reprint from _Urban Studies_, Vol. 10, No. 1, February 1973, pp. 39-68), Frank de Leeuw and Nkanta F. Ekanem, The Urban Institute, Washington, D.C., February 1974.

77. _Housing Allowances in Kansas City and Wilmington: An Appraisal_, John D. Heinberg, Peggy W. Spohn and Grace Taher, The Urban Institute, Washington D.C., May 1975 (PB 242201).

78. _The Web of Urban Housing: Analyzing Policy with a Market Simulation Model_, Frank de Leeuw and Raymond J. Struyk, The Urban Institute, Washington, D.C., 1975 (PB 249898).